Architects

of

DISASTER

Architects
of
DISASTER
The Destruction of Libya

PETE HOEKSTRA

Former Chairman, House Permanent Select
Committee on Intelligence

With Teri Blumenfeld

Foreword by
Steven Emerson
Investigative Project on Terrorism

The Calamo Press

New York | Washington DC

ISBN 978-0692438954

Investigative Project on Terrorism

The Investigative Project on Terrorism (IPT) is a nonprofit research group founded by Steven Emerson in 1995. It is recognized as the world's most comprehensive data center on radical Islamic terrorist groups. For more than a decade, the IPT has investigated the operations, funding, activities, and front groups of Islamic terrorist and extremist groups in the United States and around the world. It has become a principal source of critical evidence for a wide variety of government offices and law enforcement agencies, as well as for the U.S. Congress and numerous public policy forums. Research carried out by the IPT team has formed the basis for thousands of articles and television specials on the subject of radical Islamic involvement in terrorism and has even led to successful government action against terrorists and financiers based in the United States.

The IPT accepts no funding from outside the United States or from any governmental agency or political or religious institutions. Tax-deductible contributions should be made to its fund-raising arm, the Investigative Project on Terrorism Foundation, a 501(c)(3) tax-exempt organization.

http://www.investigativeproject.org/

Published by

 CALAMO

The Calamo Press

New York City | Washington DC

calamopress.com
Currente-Calamo LLC
2425 17th Street NW, Washington D.C. 20009
244 Fifth Avenue, Ste. D169, New York, NY 10001

ACKNOWLEDGMENTS

This book pays tribute to numerous people with whom I have worked over the years. They have invested their time and energy helping me better understand the complexities of foreign policy and national security.

But before listing them, I must first express my love and thankfulness for the greatest family imaginable. My loving and supportive wife, Diane, and our three fantastic children, Erin, Allison, and Bryan (and special daughter-in-law, Becca), all patiently accepted a life in which Dad was too often away from home. I owe a deep debt of gratitude to my wonderful parents, brothers, sisters, and in-laws, all of whom participated in eighteen years of political ups and downs. They celebrated with us, worked with us, and challenged us when we needed it. It all started with faith and family, which laid the firm foundation on which I could build my professional political career. Without my family and my faith, this never would have happened.

Now I must thank the following individuals and groups who played such an important role in my congressional career. First, I am indebted to the House leadership who appointed me to serve on the committee that I consider the most important in the U.S. House of Representatives—the House Permanent Select Committee on Intelligence. I was appointed chairman in 2004, and I served as ranking Republican from 2007 to 2011. I became privy to the most secretive aspects of our intelligence community, and I will forever remain grateful for the trust and confidence shown in me by my peers.

I express my sincerest appreciation to my staff on the Intelligence Committee during the ten years that I served, as well as those who worked in my personal congressional office. All served the committee and our country well, but I want to especially single out the two individuals who served as staff directors on the Intelligence Committee: Mike Meermans and Jim Lewis. Their years of experience in the intelligence world enabled them to quickly educate me on the finer points of spycraft. I will never forget their patience and tutoring.

I also deeply appreciate those who led my personal congressional office: Jon Vandenheuvel, Doug Koopman, John VanFossen, Amy Plaster, and Justin Wormmeester, as well as the former staffer who now represents Michigan's 2nd Congressional District, Bill Huizenga. They served the people of west Michigan with distinction and filled a void when for hours at a time I disappeared into a Sensitive Compartmental Information Facility (the SCIF) somewhere in the Capitol. There are countless others with whom I worked, including Chris Donesa, Jamal Ware, Dave Yonkman, Fred Fleitz, John Stopher, Leah Scott-Fountain, Katherine Haley, Bill Montalto, Brandi LaPerriere, Derrick Max, Jon DeWitte, Jane Jelgerhuis, Beatriz Mancilla, Jill Brown, Ashley Major, Deb Plaggemaars, Jo-Marie St. Martin, Joe diGenova, and Victoria Toensing—the list could go on and on. I thank you all, as well as the many more whom I have failed to mention.

I cannot say enough about the people of Michigan's 2nd Congressional District, who for eighteen years supported me and elected me their representative in Congress: As a Dutch-born American citizen, you enabled me to realize a true American dream, serving in the highest federally elected office I could hold as an immigrant. I firmly believe in the House and the Senate as separate but equal Houses. Thank you for giving me the opportunity to serve you and to get to know you and your families. I would not have able to write this book without all your support.

I also thank the other members of the committee with whom I served. We didn't agree on everything, but I am convinced that we all kept America's best interest the guiding light in our deliberations. I specifically call attention to the gentlewoman who served as the top Democrat on the committee during the years I served as chairman, Congresswoman Jane Harman from California. Her insights and tenacity helped us accomplish the critical work with which we were tasked. Most important, with her partnership and with that of senators Joe Lieberman and Susan Collins, we passed the landmark Intelligence Reform and Terrorism Prevention Act, which President Bush signed into law in December 2004. I consider myself fortunate to have been appointed chairman of the bipartisan House–Senate conference committee that realized a true working partnership to pass legislation that improved U.S. national security.

I extend my sincerest gratitude to the brave Americans in our intelligence community, our military, and our foreign service who sacrificed so much to promote U.S. security and values around the world. Far too many have given life or limbs to keep us safe. Others have given an abundance of scarce time and energy. In my travels around the world, you have graciously hosted and educated me in the global challenges that we face as a country, as well as in how to respond to them effectively. I have always found you committed to the United States and its interests.

The many people in Iraq, Afghanistan, Egypt, and Libya, and many others around the world, who stood and continue to stand with America—you deserve recognition as well. You supported us—often at tremendous risk—even at times when you might not have fully agreed with U.S. policies. Many among you sacrificed their own lives or livelihoods. You helped us in the face of radical jihadist terror and as the regimes of the Taliban, Saddam Hussein, and Muammar Gaddafi were overthrown. Thank you for your loyalty and support. I pay this tribute because I recognize that U.S. foreign policy has profoundly affected you. America has not always been the most reliable or dependable ally. Sometimes U.S. policy might have been misguided from the start; other times, it has shifted inconsistently. Sometimes we have forgotten our friends. To you we owe our gratitude—and, in many cases, our apologies.

And finally I must recognize Steven Emerson, Teri Blumenfeld, Robert Shillman, Jason Mintz, and the Investigative Project on Terrorism. For more than twenty years, Steven Emerson, the researchers at IPT, and IPT's supporters have led the fight to educate the American people about the very real and undiminishing threat of radical Islam. You have spoken and written with clarity about the enemy and how they exploit America's freedoms to undercut and attack us. Steve has stood at the forefront of the fight: He is the tip of the spear. Thank you for allowing me to join your team.

We hope that these pages have led you to a deeper understanding of the effects of foreign policy on U.S. national security, both for those who implement it and for those who rely on it. We hope to add value to a discussion necessary to keep America safe and forge strong alliances around the world.

— Peter Hoekstra

FOREWORD

Muammar Gaddafi ruled Libyan civilians with an iron fist for forty-two years by committing a catalogue of human rights abuses and, even more effectively, by suppressing radical Islamist terrorists both inside his country and out.

In the 1970s, Gaddafi subdued both the Sanussiyya Sufi religious order of ousted King Muhammad Idris and the Libyan chapter of the Muslim Brotherhood. He curbed the ambitions of young radicals whose organization would later become his chief antagonist—the Libyan Islamic Fighting Group (LIFG)—upon their return from fighting alongside the Afghan mujahideen against the Soviets in the 1980s. After Kabul fell in 1992, Gaddafi effectively constrained the al-Muqatila (the fighting group), a network of Libyan Afghans who had begun to plot jihad in their home country. In addition to the LIFG, groups such as the Derna Brigade, the February 17th Martyrs Brigade, the Abu Obayda Bin Aljarah Brigade, and Al Qaeda all presented persistent threats to Gaddafi's regime.

As vicious as Gaddafi was toward his countrymen, he wisely saw the fundamental flaw in engaging Islamists other than by paying groups such as Abu Nidal to wage terror campaigns on his behalf. He understood Islamists' destructive ideology, which involves killing innocent men, women, and children to achieve the goal of reestablishing the Islamic caliphate and destroying the concept of freedom wherever it exists. The Obama administration would learn that its misguided adventure in deposing Gaddafi and embracing the opposition meant unleashing the volatile forces that Gaddafi had kept under control during all the years of his rule, especially after 9/11.

We at the Investigative Project on Terrorism have been highlighting the threat of Islamist radicalism and its campaign of terror against the West for more than twenty years. We have conducted extensive research on individual jihadists, organizations, and state sponsors who played crucial roles in Libya's transformation from an international pariah to an ally in the war against radicalism, then back again to a shell state of lawlessness.

This instructive text by former House Intelligence Committee chairman and Shillman senior fellow at the Investigative Project on Terrorism Pete Hoekstra explores how the United States helped facilitate Libya's evolution and devolution over the years. Hoekstra oversaw critical aspects of American foreign policy as the chairman and, later, as the ranking Republican member on the House Intelligence Committee from 2004 to 2011. He has traveled to more than eighty countries, among them some of the most dangerous hotbeds of Islamist terror activity in the world. He approaches his subject from a depth of knowledge and a breadth of experience in the Middle East and North Africa, most notably gained in personal meetings with dictators considered among the harshest and most oppressive in the world, including Gaddafi and Syria's Bashar al-Assad.

Yes, Gaddafi was barbaric and ruthless, but he became a reliable U.S. ally who turned over his weapons of mass destruction programs in 2004 when he decided that doing so was in his best interest. He also aided in intelligence-gathering activities that led to the capture of key terrorists, thereby potentially disrupting numerous plots. But rather than continuing to support Gaddafi and his efforts, the Obama administration supported and funded known radical Islamists who murdered Gaddafi and then tore the country apart. Indeed, Obama willfully ignored elements such as the LIFG among the rebel coalition.

Hoekstra details critical dates and events such as Barack Obama's 2009 outreach to Hamas and the Egyptian Muslim Brotherhood—including by giving senior Muslim Brotherhood officials front-row seats at his speech in Cairo—as well as his siding with theological fundamentalist leaders in Iran, rather than with reformers, during the country's Green Revolution in 2009. Obama had reached out to the Islamic Front in Syria, a coalition of salafi-jihadist militias that would become the Islamic State in Iraq and Syria (ISIS). His administration also sought direct talks with Mullah Omar and the Afghani Taliban in 2011.

Hoekstra discusses how aiding the Libyan rebels in 2011 required direct cooperation with veterans of Iraq and Afghanistan, including Ansar al-Sharia. The organization's leader, Ahmed Abu Khattala, was charged as the prime suspect in the attacks on the Benghazi diplomatic compound, which resulted in the murder of U.S. Ambassador Chris Stevens, along with fellow Americans Sean Smith, Tyrone Woods, and Glen Doherty, on September 11, 2012.

U.S. foreign policy emboldened terrorists such as LIFG commander Abdel-Hakim al-Hasidi, who was responsible for multiple atrocities in the 2011 uprising; emir Abdel-Hakim Belhadj, linked to the horrific March 2004 train bombing in Madrid; and Faraj al-Chalabi, identified as a suspect in the planning of the attack on the Benghazi facility. The U.S. Department of State even paid the Muslim Brotherhood–affiliated February 17th Martyrs Brigade to provide security at Benghazi, where the group facilitated the 9/11 attack. The Obama administration, for the first time, welcomed jihadists into the U.S. coalition. They saw no difference between the good guys and the bad guys.

Today Libya, located in the soft underbelly of Europe, has become a nexus of training and equipping radicals across the Middle East and North Africa. It facilitates weapons transfers to radicals in Mali, Chad, Lebanon, Tunisia, Egypt, Syria, and Iraq. Furthermore, Obama's policy of reaching out to jihadists has given resolve to terror groups such as Boko Haram and Ansaru in Nigeria, Hamas in Gaza, and ISIS in Iraq and Syria. These are no small consequences. They all directly and indirectly affect free societies throughout the world.

Hoekstra's *Architects of Disaster* explores the mistakes that the United States has committed by engaging Islamists over the past few years, and in doing so, he helps ensure that the West need not be doomed to repeat them.

— Steven Emerson

Founder and Executive Director,

Investigative Project on Terrorism

TABLE OF CONTENTS

"I truly believe that the day I'm inaugurated, not only the country looks at itself differently, but the world looks at America differently . . . .

If I'm reaching out to the Muslim world, they understand that I've lived in a Muslim country and I may be a Christian, but I also understand their point of view . . . . My sister is half-Indonesian. I traveled there all the way through my college years. And so I'm intimately concerned with what happens in these countries and the cultures and perspective these folks have. And those are powerful tools for us to be able to reach out to the world . . . .

Then I think the world will have confidence that I am listening to them and that our future and our security is tied up with our ability to work with other countries in the world that will ultimately make us safer . . . ."

—Barack Hussein Obama, November 2007

INTRODUCTION

"You will regret it if you take a step toward intervening in our internal affairs."

—Libyan leader Muammar Gaddafi,
in a March 2011 letter to President Obama

The September 11, 2012, terrorist attack on the U.S. diplomatic compound in Benghazi that resulted in the deaths of four Americans, including Ambassador Chris Stevens, was a calamity. But it was no accident. It was the culmination of a foreign policy on Islamic terrorism that was grounded in wishful thinking and self-delusion.

The essence of that policy? That radical jihadists can be both trusted and managed—that it is possible to engage with them constructively and positively. Incredibly enough, in spite of all that has happened—especially in Libya—the Obama administration has continued this policy to the present day.

For the past few years, Libya has been very much on Americans' minds, our thinking dominated by the question of what happened in Benghazi on the terrible night of September 11, 2012—and why. And this preoccupation is natural. The murder of our ambassador and three other Americans, the likelihood that they might have been saved by more decisive action, the Obama administration's ludicrous tale that the attacks had been prompted by an obscure video, the administration's subsequent fudging and dissembling—all of it roiled our individual emotions, and quickly became the subject of fierce and bitter contention in the political arena. For conservatives, the very name "Benghazi" rightly became shorthand for an administration rife with incompetence, at ease with shocking duplicity in the defense of policies both ineffectual and deeply dishonorable. Progressives replied that Benghazi was a phony scandal—that the right's continuing fixation on it has been driven by little more than rank partisanship.

For these reasons, weeks after the 2014 midterms, the report on Benghazi by the House Intelligence Committee (which I formerly chaired) prompted giddiness among many on the left. Typically engaging in what I think of as "bunch ball," the administration's media defenders declared that the "Republican-led report" was "exhaustive" and had wholly absolved the president and his team of responsibility for the Benghazi tragedy. "G.O.P.-Led Benghazi Panel Bolsters Administration," ran the *New York Times*'s front-page headline, followed by the subhead "Democrats dismiss the investigation as an effort to discredit Hillary Rodham Clinton." "Republican-Led Report Debunks Benghazi Theories and Accusations," echoed CNN. "House Intelligence Committee's Benghazi Report Torches Conspiracy Theories," added the *Huffington Post*.

On the right, there was corresponding—and largely well-founded—disbelief and anger. Steve Hayes of the *Weekly Standard* quoted a former CIA agent who was on the ground in Benghazi that dreadful night as saying, "If this was a high school paper I would give it an F." Longtime administration critic Lindsey Graham even more pointedly described the report as being "full of crap."

In fact, the Intelligence Committee Report was not, nor did it purport to be, the definitive report on what happened in Benghazi—focusing as it did only on the period beginning with the hours immediately preceding the attack and ending a few days after it. Indeed, for all its horror, the attack on Benghazi must be seen for what it was: a snapshot of a much larger and ongoing calamity. The failures at

Benghazi reflected a failure of America's intelligence community and foreign policy apparatus of truly epic proportions, one that continues even now. As the *Washington Post* editorialized on January 13, 2015: "As 2015 begins, Libya is well on its way to becoming the Middle East's second war zone—with the same side effects of empowering radical jihadists and destabilizing neighboring countries . . . . As the situation has steadily worsened in the past two years, the Obama administration, France, Britain, and other participants in the NATO intervention have reacted not by dispatching aid but by shutting down their embassies and *washing their hands of Libya* [emphasis added]."

The sad truth is that as the cancer of global terrorism continues to metastasize, the questions about American conduct in the Middle East raised by Benghazi carry even greater weight than they did in the aftermath of that terrible night. For turning away from the lessons of Libya has vastly increased the risk that other such tragedies will occur—and on an even greater scale, threatening the very survival of the West and its values.

Again, the root of the problem is the absolute refusal of so many to appreciate the true reach and utterly ruthless nature of the jihadist threat, a mentality that has led the Obama administration not merely to refuse to explicitly name the jihadist threat, but—even more insane—also to at times tacitly embrace its most radical elements. There is no better case study of this than Libya. Indeed, as soon as I learned of the attack on the Benghazi compound, I was among those who thought it possible, even likely, that some of the jihadists involved had been trained and equipped by NATO, an analysis that has been increasingly borne out by what we've learned in the years since the attack. We're talking less about intelligence failure here than we are about naïveté run amok, forming the basis for wartime policy! And we're talking, too, about astonishing failures of judgment on the part of the president and his chief foreign policy lieutenant, Hillary Clinton—who hopes to be the *next* commander-in-chief.

It is certain that in Libya there were never any easy policy choices, let alone very many good guys—and in his day, Muammar Gaddafi had been one of the worst of the worst. Yet by the time of the war, his was the side committed to defeating the unquestionably more profound evil that is global jihad. Moreover, Gaddafi had already effectively won when, astonishingly, America weighed in to guarantee Gaddafi's defeat. The chaos that has followed should have been an obvious consequence but somehow was not and, even today, still is not to many.

In this crucial regard, Gaddafi, for all his sordid history, was infinitely wiser than Barack Obama and Hillary Clinton. Gaddafi understood the fundamental flaw of engaging Islamist terrorists. He understood their ultimate plans for all those who do not share their enthusiasm for dragging the world back to savagery and barbarism. Indeed, Gaddafi is a key figure in this story, and one too seldom mentioned—the one without whom the civil war, Benghazi, and the horrific aftermath of the spread of radical jihadism would not have unfolded at all as they actually have.

I first met Gaddafi in 2003 as part of a congressional delegation that traveled to Libya. Our visit had been specifically requested by the Bush administration to help determine whether Gaddafi was for real: Was his outreach to the West genuine? Was he really prepared to work constructively with us to defeat global jihadism?

We met with the Libyan leader for two hours, and our conclusion, Republicans and Democrats alike, was unanimous: Gaddafi was serious, and he was committed. Gravely concerned about the growing threat from radical jihadists in his own country, Gaddafi appreciated—in ways few Americans could—how vast were the jihadists' global ambitions. He readily shared his views and offered to partner with the United States to defeat our common threat.

The Sense of Congress

Congressman Sherwood Boehlert, the leader of the codel, recalled the visit in comments he made in June 2003 supporting an amendment he proposed to the Intelligence Authorization Bill, saying, "[T]hat country [Libya] is moving in the right direction. Let us hope they continue that movement. We want signals to be sent to others. We want Iran and North Korea, and other nations, others who are on the list of countries that sponsor state terrorism, to get the message; and we think this amendment that I am offering, this sense of the Congress amendment, will do the right thing in the appropriate way.

"The sense of the Congress highlighted four points:

rial activ-
ing illegal
)ying any

cal muni-
and the
have been
re facility

) departed
ing an ad-
mass de-
centrifuge
nrich ura-
sion facil-
ive SCUD-
vo partial

mittee on
se of Rep-
stant Sec-
d Compli-
hat Libya
ol for the
·'the com-
s longest
ssiles and
s declared

monitors

acts of international terrorism, including but not limited to the bombings of Pan Am Flight 103 and the La Belle Discotheque.

(b) SENSE OF CONGRESS.—It is the sense of Congress that—

(1) the world has been made safer with the dismantling and removal of Libya's weapons of mass destruction and the means to deliver them;

(2) this would not have been possible if not for decades of United States and multilateral sanctions against Libya, the demonstrated resolve of the United States in the global war on terror and the liberation of Iraq by United States and Coalition Forces;

(3) the President and previous Administrations should be commended for having the courage to undertake those policies which persuaded Libya to agree to relinquish such weapons; and

(4) other countries such as Iran, Syria, and North Korea, should follow Libya's example, and voluntarily dismantle their weapons of mass destruction and submit their programs to international inspections.

Mr. BOEHLERT (during the reading). Mr. Chairman, I ask unanimous consent that the modified amendment be considered as read and printed in the RECORD

I would eventually visit Libya twice more, on both occasions meeting with Gaddafi multiple times. My last visit was in 2008, when I traveled with a codel led by then Minority Leader John Boehner. Consequently, I witnessed up close and in person Gaddafi's rapid transition from pariah to ally—and back to pariah again.

I never for a moment forgot with whom I was dealing, always keenly aware of Gaddafi's history—but I also recognized that by then, he was an ally on whom America could count. Of course, in the end, the deal would not pay off for Gaddafi. After 2009, when new leadership in Washington fundamentally altered U.S. foreign policy, he was essentially a dead man walking, and Libya was on its way to becoming a failed state, a haven for global terrorism.

With the crucial support of Libyan jihadists, brother movements are today extending their deadly reach throughout the Middle East, Europe, and Africa. Yet even now American foreign policy continues naïvely on its way, guided by the same disastrous assumptions that led to such a calamitous end in Libya. Unless this changes—and changes quickly—even worse is surely to come.

This book looks at American foreign—and especially Middle Eastern—policy during the Obama years. It is a personal view, based on my experiences as the lead Republican on the House Intelligence Committee and, afterward, as the Shillman Senior Fellow at the Investigative Project on Terrorism. I intend in this book to lay out what happened during a particular period, highlighting the lessons that can be learned from Libya as a case study, hoping that we can build on our successes and avoid repeating our failures.

Although I recognize that serious mistakes were also made during the Bush administration, I am especially critical of the decisions made during the Obama administration, for these in particular have placed us in our current precarious and potentially disastrous situation. Specifically, Barack Obama and Hillary Clinton made three fundamental mistakes in their Libyan policy:

1. They heedlessly put in place a strategy that resulted in the overthrow of the Gaddafi government. Their approach was one that no previous administration, Democrat or Republican, had seriously considered, let alone implemented, over Gaddafi's forty-two years in power; not even after the Libyan dictator had been shown to be responsible for the notorious discotheque bombing in Munich, Germany, in 1986, and for the bombing of Pan Am Flight 103 in 1988. Moreover, President Obama and Secretary of State Clinton did so after Gaddafi had demonstrably changed his ways. The question "Why now?" is one that the president and his first secretary of state have never adequately answered.

2. Either Obama and Clinton failed to properly vet the anti-Gaddafi insurgents that America and the other NATO forces supported, or—worse (and the only plausible alternative)—they knowingly aided and abetted radical jihadist groups.

3. After Gaddafi was overthrown and Libya was broken, Obama and Clinton effectively walked away, failing to invest the resources necessary to even make possible a Libyan government friendly both to its people and to the West.

Such choices carry profound consequences, and not for Americans alone. I recall my many meetings with everyday Libyan citizens and anti-Gaddafi leaders, including their disappointment when America embraced Gaddafi, which they saw as a defeat for their dream of reform. I also saw how excited they were by the Arab Spring and, early on, by NATO's support for regime change in Libya. But I saw, too—as in their counterparts in Iraq—their hope give way to deep disappointment and increasing horror as the jihadists grew more powerful. Finally I saw how, tragically, they were left on their own when at the critical moment, America deserted them. And now the vacuum we left behind has been filled by monsters far worse than any before them.

At its conclusion, this book proposes a set of lessons whose guiding principles were sadly ignored in the run-up to and conduct of the Obama–Clinton Libyan war and its tragic aftermath—lessons that can help guide future American foreign policy. These lessons are based on a set of consistent bipartisan understandings and principles, for—if nothing else—we seem to be finally reaching consensus on one vital matter: We are all threatened by radical Islam, and it is a threat that will not soon be defeated.

What should America's long-term foreign policy objectives be? Is it wiser, in the interest of long-term stability, to seek to foster democracy and Western values in those parts of the world that have different traditions and cultures, or does it make more sense to seek merely to keep the lid on the garbage can of threats to the United States? Is there a middle ground?

These are complex questions. Although this book may not answer them in full, I hope it provides a framework for discussing them intelligently and in considerable depth.

1

GADDAFI: MAD DOG? ALLY?
OR ALL OF THE ABOVE?

When the United States took sides in the Libyan civil war in early 2011, the situation may have been murky for most Americans, casually following events in another hotspot of an endlessly troubled region—as well as for the media, whose job it was to inform them—but one thing was clear: the identity of the bad guy.

Characteristically not mincing words, Ronald Reagan had summed up the Libyan strongman in 1986 as "the mad dog of the Middle East," and few in the West saw any reason to argue. Having assumed power in a coup against King Idris in 1969, Muammar Gaddafi had not only transformed Libya into one of the world's most ruthless police states, but also made the country the world's leading sponsor of terrorism. At Gaddafi's direction, Libyan oil money underwrote groups as varied as the Provisional IRA, Uruguay's Tupamaro urban guerrillas, the Moro National Liberation Front in the Philippines, Colombia's 19th of April movement, and the Palestinian Black September group responsible for innumerable assassinations as well as the massacre of Israeli athletes at the 1972 Munich Olympic games.

However, for many, especially in America and Britain, Gaddafi's most heinous act would always be remembered as the bombing of Pan Am Flight 103 over Lockerbie, Scotland, four days before Christmas 1988, killing 243 passengers, 16 crew and 11 people on the ground. The attack was widely presumed to have been personally authorized by Gaddafi, who for years afterward resisted arrest warrants for Abdelbaset al-Megrahi, the Libyan intelligence official linked directly to the crime by investigators. Al-Megrahi was finally turned over to the UK, tried and found guilty by a three-judge panel in 2001. But in 2009, after successfully exerting pressure on the UK, Gaddafi arranged for the murderer's premature release from a British prison less than a decade later on grounds of "compassion."

Terror Attacks Attributed to Libya
(see reference notes on page 32)

May 30, 1972—Attack at Lod Airport in Israel.[a]

December 17, 1983—Vehicle bomb detonated near Harrods Department Store in Knightsbridge, London.[b]

March 16, 1984—Sudan accuses Libya of dropping five bombs from an unidentified Soviet-built bomber over Omdurman, killing five and injuring two.[c]

April 17, 1984—British police officer Yvonne Fletcher is shot and killed outside the Libyan People's Bureau in London.[d]

November 23, 1985—Hijacking of Egypt Air Flight 648, resulting in the death of dozens.[e]

December 27, 1985—Attacks against both Leonardo da Vinci–Fiumicino Airport outside Rome, Italy, and Schwechat Airport in Vienna, Austria.[f]

April 5, 1986—Libyan agents detonate a bomb in La Belle Disco in West Berlin, killing two U.S. soldiers and a Turkish woman.[g]

September 5, 1986—Hijacking of Pan Am Flight 73, killing twenty passengers.[h]

February 14, 1987—Passengers and crew are taken hostage aboard the private yacht Carin II.[i]

December 21, 1988—Terrorists detonate a bomb aboard Pan Am Flight 103 over Lockerbie, Scotland, killing 270 people.[j]

September 19, 1989—The bombing of UTA Flight 772 over Chad kills 170 passengers and crew.[k]

Muammar
Al Gathafi

The
Green
Book

Part one
The solution to the problem
of Democracy
Part two
The solution to
the Economic Problem
Part three
The Social Basis of
the Third Universal Theory

Gaddafi's personal behavior only confirmed his sordid reputation. Over his forty-two-year reign, there came regular reports of his systematic brutalization of women, including persistent charges that he'd raped literally hundreds of teenage girls, as well as his female bodyguards. Consumed by paranoia, Gaddafi was at the same time megalomaniacal. He proclaimed his *Green Book*—Gaddafi's answer to Mao's *Little Red Book* and compulsory reading in Libya—to be "the guide to the emancipation of man."

According to noted historian Andrew Roberts, the three following quotations are characteristic of the sort of "wisdom" on offer in the book:

- "Women, like men, are human beings. This is an incontestable truth . . . . Women are different from men in form because they are females, just as all females in the kingdom of plants and animals differ from the male of their species . . . . According to gynecologists, women, unlike men, menstruate each month . . . . Since men cannot be impregnated, they do not experience the ailments that women do. She breastfeeds for nearly two years."

- "There are inevitable cycles of social history: the yellow race's domination of the world, when it came from Asia, and the white race's attempts at colonizing extensive areas of all continents of the world. Now it is the turn of the black race to prevail in the world."

- "Although it is democratically not permissible for an individual to own any information or publishing medium, all individuals have a natural right to self-expression by any means, even if such means were insane and meant to prove a person's insanity."

"I find," President Reagan contemptuously observed of the Libyan dictator, "he's not only a barbarian, but he's flaky."

The American public had all this in mind, along with much more, when reports came, in the wake of the so-called Arab Spring that had brought down long-established governments in Egypt and Tunisia, that anti-Gaddafi, supposedly "pro-democracy," protests had broken out across Libya. After Gaddafi responded to the demonstrators with characteristic brutality, the country erupted in full-fledged civil war.

However, it was soon apparent that in this new shooting war, the "rebels" were no match for Gaddafi's military. Driven by ever more horrific reports of government atrocities against the civilian population, the United States, Britain, and France hastily put together a UN resolution instituting a "no-fly zone," "flight ban," and freezing of assets designed to neutralize Gaddafi's air power and government.

Having been assumed without the consent of Congress, America's role in the conflict generated controversy from the start, with elected representatives across the political spectrum condemning the president's unilateral action. Liberal Democrat Dennis Kucinich went so far as to suggest that Mr. Obama might be impeached for violation of the War Powers Act, and Michigan Republican Representative Candice Miller spoke for many when she presciently observed that

Obama had "failed to state a clear and convincing explanation of the vital national interest at stake which demands our intervention in Libya . . . [and] failed to state a clearly defined mission for our military to defend that interest." On June 3, by a 268–145 vote, the House passed House Resolution 292, asserting that the "President has failed to provide Congress with a compelling rationale" for the Libya action, adding that "[the] President shall not deploy, establish, or maintain the presence of units and members of the United States Armed Forces on the ground in Libya unless the purpose of the presence is to rescue a member of the Armed Forces from imminent danger." But there was also support for the campaign from leading figures on both sides of the aisle, among them senators John McCain and Joseph Lieberman, as well as Senate Foreign Relations Committee chairman John Kerry, who warned that "the international community cannot simply watch from the sidelines as this quest for democracy is met with raw violence."

Unsurprisingly, public opinion polls fluctuated somewhat during the course of the operation, but generally speaking, clear majorities of Americans—though adamantly opposed to any introduction of American ground forces—ultimately supported the low-risk air operation. Although the United States saw sporadic anti-war protests in large cities and university towns, none approached the scale of those that had taken place during the Bush years, focusing on the U.S. invasion of Iraq.

As the war continued during the following weeks and months, and as NATO increasingly threw in on behalf of the insurgents— flying more than 9,700 strike sorties and providing some 20,000 tons of American-sanctioned Qatari weapons—the odds on the ground steadily shifted in the "rebels'" favor. Indeed, it is certain that absent NATO participation, Gaddafi would have prevailed—and equally certain that NATO would not have intervened in the absence of American participation.[1]

By October 2011, Gaddafi was on the run. When the convoy in which he was attempting to flee Libya was bombed, he fled on foot. Cornered while hiding in a drainpipe, "the Mad Dog of the Middle East" was summarily executed by his country's supposed liberators, his body afterward paraded through the streets. Gruesome though the spectacle was, it's a safe bet that few American tears were shed on his behalf.

Indeed, the chief celebrant of Gaddafi's murder was America's secretary of state, Hillary Clinton, who actually gloated on camera: "We came, we saw, he died."

It is an image that will likely haunt her presidential campaign—and should.

For, of course, there was far more to the story than much of the American public—and, tragically, the president and his top foreign policy aide—seemed to grasp.

Notes for "Terror attacks attributed to Libya" (see page 26)

An index of linked footnote references can be found at
http://www.architectsofdisaster.com/footnotes/.

a   "Foreign Claims Settlement Commission Libya Claims Program," U.S. Department of Justice.

b   Ibid.

c   "Plane Bombs the Sudan, Which Accuses Libyans," *New York Times*, March 16, 1984.

d   Leon Watson and Martin Robinson, "Parents of Murdered WPC Yvonne Fletcher Lay Flowers at Spot Where She Was Shot Dead 30 Years Ago as 'MI6 Spies Close in on Prime Suspect,'" *Daily Mail*, April 16, 2014.

e   "Foreign Claims Settlement Commission Libya Claims Program," U.S. Department of Justice.

f   Brian Lee Davis, "Qaddafi , Terrorism, and the Origins of the U.S. Attack on Libya," Greenwood Publishing Group, 1990, p. 80.

g   LCDR Joseph T. Stanik, USN (Ret.), "HH 362—History of the Middle East," U.S. Naval Academy, April 2002.

h   Arun Venugopal, "Post-Gadhafi, Survivors of Pan Am Flight 73 Seek Compensation," WNYC, November 27, 2011.

i   Michael Kirkland, "Libya Hostage-Taking Suit Still Alive," UPI, April 22, 2003.

j   "Pan Am Flight 103: A Look Back at the Lockerbie Bombing," *New York Daily News*, December 23, 2013.

k   Kimberly Kindy, "Families of Americans Killed in 1989 Bombing See Victory over Libya Nullified," *Washington Post*, December 23, 2008.

2

THE REST OF THE STORY

Yes, Muammar Gaddafi was a monster, but he was our monster. In the ways that mattered most, he was preferable—immensely so—to many of those who brought him down, and the stability of Libya under his control was preferable to the chaos that has followed. Although NATO effectively brought down Gaddafi, it broke Libya but didn't own it or do anything to fix it.

The fact is, in the decade following September 11, 2001, Gaddafi had emerged as one of America's greatest assets in one of the world's most dangerous regions, northern Africa—strategically located between the tinder box of the Sahel and the soft underbelly of southern Europe. Libya had become a stabilizing force in a very delicate and important region of the world.

Although for several years Gaddafi had been inching his way toward reconciliation with the West in hopes of escaping the economic sanctions that were strangling the Libyan economy, his dramatic shift in the wake of the terrorist attacks on New York and Washington that terrible day was nothing short of stunning. Indeed, his conversion from bellicose adversary to tacit ally was perhaps the greatest early triumph of the Bush administration's uncompromising response to international terrorism. Although Gaddafi was obviously driven by his instinct for self-preservation, his change of heart was also the fruit of a consistent policy of firmness and resolve that had marked American foreign policy over multiple administrations, Republican and Democrat alike.

So terrified was Gaddafi in the period after the 9/11 attacks that Libya might now be in America's sights that, according to a declassified U.S. diplomatic cable, the Libyan dictator "sounded hysterical in his telephone call to [Jordan's] King Abdullah . . . as if only the King's personal intervention would prevent U.S. action." Publicly, Gaddafi loudly condemned the 9/11 terror attacks and called for American–Libyan cooperation in the fight against Al Qaeda. A year and a half later, when American-led coalition forces toppled Iraqi dictator Saddam Hussein, Italian press accounts quoted Prime Minister Silvio Berlusconi as saying that a fearful Gaddafi told him over the phone, "Tell them I will do whatever they want."[2]

By then, American–Libyan cooperation was already well under way. The month after 9/11, Assistant Secretary of State William J. Burns, along with Ben Bonk, deputy director of the CIA's counter-terrorism center, flew to London to meet with Libyan intelligence chief Moussa Koussa. Koussa reportedly provided the names of Libyan Islamist operatives who trained in Afghanistan, as well as detailed information about leaders of the Libyan Islamic Fighting Group (LIFG) who were living in Britain—information said to be a windfall for the CIA in its hunt for jihadists.

Koussa, whom I met on each of my three congressional delegation trips to Libya, was, like so many in the region, a complex and contradictory figure, a man at once immensely personable and yet who had much blood on his hands. Born in 1947, he was a graduate of Michigan State, and he loved following MSU basketball, especially MSU graduate Magic Johnson and coach Tom Izzo, whom he hoped one day to meet. Yet he was a key advisor to Gaddafi when the dictator was at his worst, and he moved steadily upward through the ranks, from security specialist for Libyan embassies in Europe to, ultimately, head of the Libyan intelligence service, serving as a key member of the dictator's inner circle. Even in his role as director of the World Centre for Resistance to Imperialism, in charge of propagating the Gaddafi revolution worldwide, it is unlikely that he ever left the Libyan intelligence agency, Jamahiriya el-Mukhabarat—and reliable intelligence sources have accused Koussa of direct responsibility for the regime's most heinous crimes: the 1988 Lockerbie bombing of Pan Am Flight 103, which killed 270; the 1989 bombing of UTA Flight 772, which killed 170; and the bombing of a German disco, which killed two U.S. soldiers and a Turkish woman.[3] He later helped secure the release of convicted Lockerbie bomber Abd al-Basit Ali Meghrahi, who was serving a life sentence, on the grounds of his ill health.[4]

Yet Koussa was also a key figure in the normalization of relations between Libya, Britain, and the United States.[5]

American negotiators made it clear that any new Libyan–American partnership was predicated on Gaddafi's payment of compensation to the families of the Lockerbie victims, as well as on Libyan termination of its weapons of mass destruction (WMD) programs. For nearly two years, Gaddafi balked at these requirements, fearful that acknowledging responsibility for Lockerbie would be perceived by his enemies at home and abroad as a sign of weakness. But Gaddafi eventually relented after receiving assurances that the United States and Britain were prepared to fully normalize relations. In August 2003, he agreed to pay the Lockerbie families $2.7 billion.

Four months later, he made the stunning announcement that he was surrendering his WMD programs. In 1997, Libya had purchased twenty pre-assembled L-1 centrifuges, along with components for an additional 200 L-1 centrifuges, through the proliferation network of Pakistani nuclear scientist Abdul Qadeer Khan. It also imported equipment for a large precision machine shop to build centrifuges, as well as small quantities of UF6 (uranium hexafluoride) for use as feedstock for enrichment. In 2000, it acquired two L-2 centrifuges and ordered components for building 10,000 more through the A. Q. Khan network. But now, at Gaddafi's request, American and British teams entered the country and disabled or removed all of Libya's centrifuges and other dual-use nuclear equipment.

Inching toward Diplomatic Normalcy

April 5, 1999—Pursuant to a deal negotiated by the UN Secretary General and other high-profile intermediaries, Libya extradites the two suspects in the 1988 bombing of Pan Am Flight 103 to Scottish authorities in the Netherlands for trial in a Scottish court. The UN suspends sanctions against Libya.

July 1999—Britain and Libya resume diplomatic relations.

December 1999—Gaddafi denounces terrorism, having already expelled the Abu Nidal terrorist organization and closed terrorist training camps.

May 3, 2000—The trial of the suspects in the Pan Am Flight 103 bombing opens. The two suspects, Abd al-Basit Ali Meghrahi and Al-Amin Khalifa Fahima, plead not guilty.

January 31, 2001—The Scottish court in the Netherlands finds Abd al-Basit Ali Megrahi guilty and sentences him to life in prison. The court acquits Al-Amin Khalifa Fahima. The Bush administration states that it will neither support the permanent lifting of UN sanctions nor consider the resumption of normal relations until the Libyan government accepts full responsibility for the destruction of Pan Am Flight 103 and pays damages to the families of the victims.

September 12, 2003—In a 13–0 vote, the UN Security Council formally lifts sanctions on Libya. The United States and France abstain. The Security Council's action follows Libya's August

15 agreement to compensate the victims of the Pan Am Flight 103 bombing, as well as Tripoli's formal acceptance of responsibility for that bombing.[6]

January 18, 2004—U.S. and British officials arrive in Libya to begin eliminating and removing WMD designs and stockpiles.[7]

February 6, 2004—A U.S.-led delegation meets with Libyan officials in London "to begin a political dialogue about the future of U.S.–Libyan relations."[8]

February 12, 2004—Former House Intelligence Committee chairman Pete Hoekstra participates in the first of three congressional delegations to meet with Gaddafi in Libya. The State Department asks Hoekstra and other members of the delegation to express the United States' gratitude for Libya's having abandoned its WMD programs and having renounced its ties to terror groups.

February 26, 2004—The United States lifts its Libya travel ban. U.S. citizens are allowed to spend money in Libya, and businesses may enter negotiations to reacquire presanctions holdings inside Libya. The United States also offers Libya the possibility of opening a diplomatic interests section in Washington.[9]

March 5, 2004—Libyan officials submit a complete declaration of the state's chemical weapons stockpile and facilities.

September 20, 2004—The United States lifts most of its remaining sanctions on Libya.

May 15, 2006—Secretary of State Condoleezza Rice announces the establishment of full diplomatic relations between the United States and Libya.[10]

October 16, 2007—Libya gains a seat on the UN Security Council.[11]

January 3, 2008—U.S. and Libyan officials sign their first bilateral agreement, the Science and Technology Cooperation Agreement.[12]

August 14, 2008—The United States and Libya sign the U.S.–Libya Claims Settlement Agreement, providing full compensation for victims of the Lockerbie bombing and the bombing of the Berlin disco.[13]

September 5, 2008—Rice meets with Gaddafi, becoming the highest-ranking U.S. official to visit Libya in more than fifty years.

In return, the Bush administration began steadily normalizing relations. In February 2004, it lifted the ban on Americans' traveling to Libya and reopened the U.S. interest section in Tripoli, which was upgraded to a liaison office four months later. In September 2004, the administration lifted most trade sanctions against Libya, and by 2005 American oil contractors were active and productive.

In May 2006, Secretary of State Condoleezza Rice announced that the United States was removing Libya's designation as a state sponsor of terrorism and restoring full diplomatic relations with Gaddafi "in recognition of Libya's continued commitment to its renunciation of terrorism and the excellent cooperation Libya has provided to the United States and other members of the international community in response to common global threats faced by the civilized world since September 11, 2001." In other words—an ally.

CONDOLEEZZA RICE'S VISIT OPENS NEW ERA IN US–LIBYA RELATIONS

By Tim Butcher, Middle East Correspondent
The Daily Telegraph
September 5, 2008

Miss Rice said her visit proved Washington was prepared to forgive former enemies, even ones like Libya that perpetrated acts of terrorism that cost American lives.

By flying to Tripoli and shaking the hand of Colonel Gaddafi, Miss Rice effectively ended three decades of hostility between the oil-rich desert nation and America, an

Condoleezza Rice and Muammar Gaddafi meet in Tripoli. Photo: AFP

enmity that claimed lives in the 1980s when Libyan-backed terrorists perpetrated attacks such as the Lockerbie bombing.

"This demonstrates that the U.S. doesn't have permanent enemies," Miss Rice said. "It demonstrates that when countries are prepared to make strategic changes in direction, the United States is prepared to respond. Quite frankly I never thought I would be visiting Libya and so it is quite something."

The value of that cooperation can hardly be overstated. As Gaddafi began implementing his disarmament pledge in the spring of 2004, the CIA opened an office in Libya, and intelligence cooperation between Washington and Tripoli grew rapidly. In addition to providing extensive information to the CIA about Libyan nationals in Al Qaeda, the regime gave Washington a treasure trove of information about black market suppliers, front companies, and other elements of the A.Q. Khan nuclear proliferation network. According to Kenneth Katzman, a terrorism analyst at the Congressional Research Service, information provided by the Libyans "helped us to track down aspects of the black-market network and contributed to the shutdown of parts of that network in Malaysia and the United Arab Emirates."[14] "The international community's understanding of the global black market in the world's most dangerous technologies was aided considerably by the revelations that flowed from the Libyan program," Assistant Secretary of State William J. Burns told Congress in March 2005.[15]

Gaddafi also used his regime's extensive contacts in Africa to aid the U.S. war on terror. The Libyan leader invested heavily in African countries facing Islamist security threats and provided valuable financial support to African Union peacekeepers combating Islamists in Somalia. When rebels in Chad captured Ammari Saifi, a leader of the Algerian Salafist Group for Preaching and Combat (SGPC), the Libyans pressured the rebels to hand him over to Algerian authorities—reportedly going as far as to threaten air strikes—and helped arrange the transfer in mid-2004. In 2010, Gaddafi provided reconnaissance airplanes to Mali to support its fight against Al Qaeda–linked Islamist rebels.[16]

Within a few years, U.S.–Libyan intelligence cooperation reached a level comparable in many respects to U.S. partnerships with long-standing Arab allies. At least three Libyan-born terror suspects claim that they were interrogated in Guantanamo by visiting Libyan intelligence agents.[17] The Bush administration rendered back to Libya at least fourteen Libyan terrorist suspects in its custody or that of allies—most of them Libyan Islamic Fighting Group members and all but one a veteran of the war in Afghanistan.[18] In 2005, the CIA reportedly agreed to provide counterterrorism training to Libyan agents.[19]

Gaddafi's intelligence cooperation became even more invaluable when Libyan jihadists flocked to Iraq to fight U.S.-led coalition forces. In contrast to the Saudis, the Libyan leader did not undercut his cooperation in the war on terror by turning a blind eye to jihadist infiltration of Iraq or by spending billions of dollars promoting the spread of radical Wahhabi Islamist ideology around the world.

Although the Bush administration's reconciliation with Tripoli was criticized for privileging security interests over human rights concerns, human rights conditions in Libya generally improved during this period. In mid-2005, Gaddafi allowed Human Rights Watch to enter the country for a lengthy visit to examine conditions first-hand. The organization subsequently released a report that characterized Gaddafi's Libya as "a country undergoing gradual change after years of strict repression and global isolation."[20]

This was the Gaddafi, and the Libya, inherited by the Obama administration after the 2008 presidential elections: a Libya that was stable, and a Gaddafi no longer in the garbage can but, to the contrary, helping to keep the lid on the threat posed by radical jihadists.

But with radically different thinking in the White House, neither a stable Libya nor Gaddafi would survive Obama's first term. Neither would the American ambassador, nor three other Americans.

3

A NEW DAY: EMBRACING "MODERATE" JIHADISTS

As he never stopped stressing in the run-up to the 2008 election and even afterward, Barack Obama was going to be a different kind of president. From the outset, in speech after speech and policy initiative after policy initiative, that is how he defined himself: as the polar opposite of his predecessor. And in no arena was this more the case than that of his positions on the Middle East and the war on terror. As he stated in New Hampshire in 2007, the world would view America fundamentally differently when he was president. He would not let the United States act unilaterally. He would resist the impulse to put boots on the ground. He would bring home those already there. He would close Gitmo! And he would address the threat posed by the global jihadist network not with blunt force, but rather by fostering cooperation with more "moderate" Islamists.

By doing all this, Obama was certain that he would change hearts and minds, rolling back long-festering (and, in his view, well-earned) anti-American and anti-West sentiment in the region. Such a strategy meant curtailing heavy surveillance of mosques, wiretaps, and other established—and highly effective—means of nipping terrorist plots in the bud. The idea was that doing so would win cooperation from Muslim American organizations and communities; abroad, would-be terrorists would be persuaded to choose politics over violence.

Key to such an approach was that rather than reflexively supporting secular (or, at any rate, anti-radical Islamist) dictators, the Obama administration would actively engage with those Islamists whom it deemed "moderate." This was a fundamental and radical shift of policy, and it would be years before its ramifications would be fully understood.

The administration's definition of "moderate" was soon shown to be astonishingly broad: It often involved nothing more than a group's professed commitment to nonviolence, however unsavory the group's ultimate objectives. Among the groups with whom the administration believed America could do business were some, like Egypt's powerful Muslim Brotherhood, that had been pointedly shunned by all previous administrations. Indeed, in an administration obsessed with appearances, it was hardly happenstance that six months into Obama's administration, in June 2009, key members of the Muslim Brotherhood were positioned in the front row for the president's landmark speech in Cairo.

Divided into seven sections—violent extremism, the Israeli–Palestinian conflict, nuclear weapons, democracy, religious freedom, women's rights, and economic development—the Cairo speech was titled "A New Beginning," and it stressed the bonds between America and the Muslim world. Obama spoke of his own childhood in Muslim Indonesia, of the Muslim world's contributions to the arts and sciences, and of prominent Muslim Americans, such as Muhammad Ali and Malcolm X. On the topic of Iraq, the president said that recent events had "reminded America of the need to use diplomacy and build international consensus to resolve our problems whenever possible," pledging to "remove combat troops from Iraqi cities by July, and to remove all of our troops from Iraq by 2012."

"Be conscious of God," he quoted the Qur'an, "and always speak the truth." Hardly incidentally, just two days before the Cairo speech, the president had confirmed on NPR that he would also welcome dialogue with the terrorist movement Hamas so long as its leaders recognized "that they can achieve their aims more effectively through political means."[21]

As Director of National Intelligence James R. Clapper explained to a congressional committee as late as February, 2012, Al Qaeda would "find it difficult to compete for local support with groups like the Muslim Brotherhood that participate in the political process, provide social services and advocate religious values." But what in fact happened in 2014 with the rise of ISIS is that Al Qaeda found it difficult to compete with even more radical jihadist groups.

Obama's remarkably forgiving—and all too trusting—attitude toward these groups at least in part reflected his administration's view that the United States had to face up to the stark reality that accommodation of Islamists was inescapable in light of their clout in the Arab–Islamic world. But it unquestionably also spoke to the sense, so prevalent in the faculty lounge from which the president and many in his circle had emerged, that the United States had long been a malignant rather than a benevolent force in the underdeveloped world, with much to own up to. Thus it is that in his public pronouncements and his administration's actions, Obama has often seemed determined—sometimes even desperate—to present himself to the world's 1.5 billion Sunni Muslims as a sympathetic figure who bears them only goodwill.

Soon after assuming office, President Obama began reaching out to Hamas and the Muslim Brotherhood, and—as noted by former UK ambassador Charles Crawford—his Cairo speech capped this new approach: "On June 4, 2009, Obama delivered a speech to the Muslim world in Cairo in which he declared that 'America and Islam are not exclusive.'"[22] What this really meant, Crawford paraphrased, was: "Under my restrained leadership the United States will respect and accept conservative forms of Islam. Even if Islamism gets too aggressive we don't plan to do much about it. And we may not be too active in supporting Muslim liberal trends either. Steady as she goes. And btw I do hope you have noticed that I am not G. W. Bush."[23]

This was the backdrop to American support of the "rebels" against Gaddafi. Though Obama waited until hundreds of U.S. diplomats and civilians had been evacuated on February 25, 2011, to impose unilateral sanctions and explicitly call for Gaddafi to step down, it is now clear that Obama's goal from the start was that the Libyan rebellion fully succeed.[24]

What is striking is that this required direct cooperation with a force counting among its number countless salafi-jihadist veterans of the global Al Qaeda network, with American policymakers seemingly content to buy jihadists' assurances that they would pursue jihad solely in their homeland, afterward laying down their arms.

In brief, for the first time, American policymakers willingly made the distinction between "good" jihadists—those entitled to the support indispensable to their fight—and "bad" jihadists, who even now were regular targets of American drone attacks in Afghanistan and Pakistan. Of course, ideologically, and in their ultimate goals (notwithstanding professions to the contrary), the "good" and "bad" jihadists were close to identical. And both the "good" and "bad" were well aware, even if the Americans were not, that according to their interpretation of the Qur'an, lying to infidels in the service of the cause was not merely permissible, but in fact encouraged.

TAQIYYA

Taqiyya explains how adherents to Islam—a self-professed religion of peace—justify their role in the vast majority of terror attacks around the world.[25]

Taqiyya offers two basic uses. The better known of the two—historically practiced by Shi'i communities—involves dissembling over one's religious identity when in fear of persecution. The other—largely practiced by Sunni communities—enables Muslims to actively lie about their religion when waging jihad against infidels.[26]

Islamists interpret their scripture to mean that they are allowed to lie about the nature of Islam to further their political goals. This idea is based upon Islamist interpretations of the peace treaty signed between Mohammad and the Quraysh tribe in Mecca—which, though signed as a ten-year truce, was annulled by Mohammad two years into the deal, after which he conquered Mecca.

For example, in 2012, during riots outside the U.S. embassy in Cairo, the Muslim Brotherhood tweeted messages of support and solidarity in English even while using Arabic messages to exhort their supporters to riot. Iran is widely suspected of utilizing taqiyya in its negotiations with the United States, in a bid to deceitfully obtain nuclear weapons.[27]

Yet in Obama's worldview, America was engaged not in "a boundless 'global war on terror,' but rather [in] . . . a series of persistent targeted efforts to dismantle specific networks of violent extremists that threaten America,"[28] as the president himself put it. Thus, it was essential to make a "distinction between the capacity and reach of a bin Laden and a network that is actively planning major terrorist plots against the homeland versus jihadists who are engaged in various local power struggles and disputes, often sectarian."[29]

It was such thinking that led the Obama administration to seek direct talks with Mullah Omar and the Afghani Taliban in 2011[30] and, even more astonishing in retrospect, to reach out to the Islamic Front in Syria,[31] the coalition of salafi-jihadist militias that in December 2013 would metastasize into ISIS.

Although early in his presidency Obama signaled his greater acceptance of radical jihadism by siding with the Iranian regime over pro-democracy protestors during the Green Revolution, as well as with Egypt's Muslim Brotherhood—both in 2009—the full extent of the transformation of American engagement with the Islamists only became fully apparent in Libya. Indeed, Libya ought to have put this policy of wishful thinking to the test—and then to an end. For in Libya, where many supposed U.S. allies made only the thinnest pretense at political moderation or a readiness to embrace democratic norms, the consequences were all too quickly apparent.

Still, even with the evidence before them, Obama's team characteristically remained obdurate, maintaining that their approach was isolating the real foe. "Al Qaeda seeks to portray America as an enemy of the world's Muslims," John O. Brennan, assistant to the president for homeland security and counterterrorism, explained in June 2011, midway through the Libyan civil war. But, he said, America's action on behalf of the "rebels" had made it "clear that the United States is not, and never will be, at war with Islam," thereby eroding "the ability of Al Qaeda and its network to inspire people."[32] Without any precondition, jihadists were welcomed into America's coalition for the first time.

4

CHANGING SIDES

How were the members of the president's team able to persuade themselves of what now is seen as such a self-evident fiction? How did leading Obama administration figures, from Secretary of State Hillary Clinton on down, having full access to intelligence indicating that the forces arrayed against Muammar Gaddafi numbered a great many committed jihadist militants, delude themselves into believing that these zealots could be not merely managed, but in fact trusted?

Certainly there were many others involved in the rebellion who harbored far more noble hopes and goals for a post-Gaddafi regime. Nonetheless, it should have been clear from the outset that should the rebellion succeed, the inclusion of so many elements committed to jihad, battle-hardened and well armed, would make the rebuilding of Libya highly unlikely, if not bordering on the impossible.

Moreover, in contrast—and this was the most compelling reason not to become involved in a Libyan civil war—no matter what the United States thought of the Libyan dictator and his long, ugly history, he had proven himself a model ally in America's war against terrorism. Although Gaddafi's crushing of the fledgling rebellion, had he been allowed to do so, would indeed have been a brutal and ugly business, far from threatening America's national interest, it ultimately would have served it.

Looking back, the decision should not have been even a close call. This was not nearly so agonizing a quandary as, for instance, that faced by American decision makers of an earlier generation considering whether to support the mujahideen fighting the invading Soviets in Afghanistan—a decision, that is, about which of two evils ultimately stood to do us greater harm. In this case, the only potential threat to American geopolitical interests lay in a victory by Gaddafi's adversaries.

Then again, as the rebellion took hold, the analogy Obama and his advisors had in mind was not so much Afghanistan as Kosovo. As in the Balkans in 1998, the justification for intervention was entirely to avoid what they deemed an impending humanitarian calamity.

Keenly aware of this, the anti-Gaddafi insurgents astutely cast themselves early on as the beleaguered Libyan branch of the vaunted "Arab Spring," the supposed awakening of democratic yearnings in the Muslim world that had generated such excitement and hope in the West and that had already produced successful popular uprisings in Tunisia and Egypt. (This latter, however, would prove illusory, temporarily ushering into power the Islamist Muslim Brotherhood.) In this scenario, the "rebels" were presented in the Western media as patriots seeking justice and self-determination, with Gaddafi cast as the blood-thirsty tyrant capable of any atrocity in his mania to cling to power. And in light of his history, the Libyan dictator was ideally cast in the role. Nonetheless, the media's idealization—and whitewashing—of the other side's darker character and motives was a dereliction of journalistic duty.

The contrast with Kosovo is instructive. No matter what one thought of the Clinton administration's decision to intervene in the Balkans in 1998—and at the time it was highly controversial— there was no question about its objective: to end a proven ongoing genocide. But in this case, humanitarian concerns would turn out to be largely illusory, merely pretexts for an intervention leading to regime change.

However, even the president's inner circle was divided over the question of Libyan intervention, with then Secretary of Defense Robert Gates and then Director of Central Intelligence Leon Panetta arguing strenuously against American involvement—as they also opposed Obama's disastrous decision to leave no residual American force in Iraq. On the other side were Secretary of State Clinton and influential presidential advisor and future UN Ambassador Samantha Power, a classic academic liberal whose book *A Problem from Hell*, dealing with the failure of the West to stop genocide in Uganda, had deeply impressed Obama.

Competitive/Red Team Analysis—How to Make Better Decisions

Competitive, or Red Team, analysis ranks among the most effective tools for policymakers. It enables them to hear competing viewpoints when evaluating various options.

Red Teaming involves viewing a problem from the perspective of a competitor to enhance decision-making. It largely applies to security, but it can be applied much more broadly to include corporate settings and other situations in need of a challenge to conventional thinking.[33]

We initiated Red Team analysis during the evaluation of a major government satellite program during my time as chairman of the House Intelligence Committee. The committee asked a group of independent experts to find out why the program continuously experienced delays in its implementation. The outside experts concluded that government overseers had too optimistically projected outcomes, that technical hurdles would remain significant, that we should expect more costly delays, and that the technology might never work. Based on the Red Team analysis, we decided to kill the program.

I often wonder whether the Obama administration incorporated any Red Team analysis to evaluate the various strategies under consideration for Libya's future. Did they solicit any independent alternative to their own worldview? Did they seek a better understanding by asking for opposing views on the potential ramifications of engaging with jihadists? The evidence suggests that they did not—yet doing so could have meant a world of difference in how they approached a foreign policy decision that would have such enormous consequences.

After the disastrous consequences of the administration's Libyan policy had become all too clear—and with Hillary Clinton gearing up for a presidential run—many speculated about why Hillary had been so heedlessly zealous a proponent of the administration's Libyan policy. In seeking an answer, Paul Mirengoff of the respected blog *PowerLine* cites "Joseph Miller—the pen name for a high ranking Defense Department official," who wrote in the *Daily Caller* that "Clinton's husband, former President Bill Clinton, describes his failure to intervene in the Rwanda genocide as the lowest moment of his presidency. Bearing that in mind, Secretary Clinton did not want a similar event to occur on her watch as secretary of state, because she intended to run for the presidency in 2016 and didn't want to give her challengers any ammunition to use against her. So she decided to push for action despite the advice against doing so by her colleagues at CIA and the Pentagon." Adds Mirengoff: "This is speculation, of course. But it's difficult to discern a better explanation."

No matter the reason, it proved a grievous error—one that Hillary herself saw, in the wake of the Benghazi tragedy, as something that might well come back to haunt her during a 2016 presidential run. Little wonder that she was so desperately eager to declare, in the soon-to-be infamous construction, "What difference, at this point, does it make?" No wonder that her Praetorian Guard in the mainstream press has similarly sought to consistently downplay not only Ms. Clinton's initial insistence that the terrorist attack was the result of an obscure movie, but also, in a broader sense, what Ms. Clinton's role in formulating Libyan policy says about the quality of her leadership and judgment.

Indeed, although she has since made strenuous efforts to distance herself from Barack Obama's terrorism policies, the former secretary of state was front and center promoting the administration's strenuous efforts to ensure that nothing in the American tradition be taken as an affront to Islam—and, indeed, to ensure that those seen as attacking Islamic values be marginalized. As John O'Sullivan pointed out in the *Wall Street Journal,* in 2011, as part of a dialogue "with the 56 states of the Organization of the Islamic Conference, which is seeking an international law prohibiting blasphemy," Hillary "told the OIC that, while the First Amendment prevented the U.S. from prohibiting speech, the administration might still 'use some old-fashioned techniques of peer pressure and shaming so that people don't feel they have the support to do what we abhor.'"

Although the president himself initially had grave reservations about intervening in Libya, Secretary Clinton's position began to hold sway after the second week of March, when it became clear that the tide of the war was turning in Gaddafi's favor. Even then, determined as always to minimize the political risks and to throw as sharp a contrast as possible with the policies of his predecessor, Obama insisted that any U.S. military action be multilateral, UN-sanctioned, and explicitly endorsed by the Arab League (an unprecedented move). Clinton and U.S. Ambassador to the UN Susan Rice, a fellow proponent of military intervention, managed to bring these conditions about in a matter of days.[34]

UN Resolution 1973 authorized member states "to take all necessary measures" short of ground forces to enforce a no-fly zone and arms embargo "to protect civilians and civilian populated areas under threat of attack" in Libya.[35] U.S. officials vehemently insisted that this was the sole objective of the NATO air campaign that ensued.

Yet from the start the Obama administration was highly flexible in its interpretation of Resolution 1973. When regime forces proved far more resilient than expected in blunting rebel advances, the resolution was interpreted as allowing air strikes against any and all combatants fighting for Gaddafi, regardless of whether they posed a threat to civilians. NATO used Resolution 1973 as justification for pummeling entrenched Libyan defenders until they abandoned their positions.[36] Even more striking, the administration targeted Gaddafi personally on the grounds that as head of the Libyan military, he was in charge of command and control. Indeed, even with the Libyan strongman on the run (and thus no longer in command and control of anything), on October 20, administration officials interpreted Resolution 1973 as justifying the bombing of his personal convoy. It was the last NATO air strike of the war, and it resulted in Gaddafi's murder by rebels while he was being held in custody.

All this was unprecedented. The longest-established condition for UN-sanctioned military intervention, formally enshrined in the UN Charter, is to counter a major threat to international peace. Yet Gaddafi's Libya had ended its WMD programs in the mid-2000s, and it had not been linked to international terrorist groups since the 1990s. Moreover, the country enjoyed warm relations with its neighbors.

The only other widely accepted justification for foreign military intervention is the prevention of egregious human rights abuses— and even here the case was far from clear. Although, for instance,

Human Rights Watch had reported the killing of eighty-four unarmed demonstrators by the Gaddafi regime before February 19, that number paled in comparison to the 846 Egyptian civilians who had been killed in just eleven days a few weeks earlier—and the Obama administration wasn't calling for intervention in Egypt. (Ultimately the Mubarak regime was overthrown in Egypt, but not through direct NATO and U.S. intervention.)

Undeterred, President Obama took the position that Libya faced a "looming humanitarian crisis" threatening to stain "the conscience of the world"—that the U.S. could not "wait for the images of slaughter and mass graves before taking action."[37] "We were looking at 'Srebrenica on steroids'—the real or imminent possibility that up to a hundred thousand people could be massacred, and everyone would blame us for it," White House Middle East advisor Dennis Ross told a group of foreign policy experts after the intervention began.[38] The administration argued not so much that systemic human rights abuses were in progress, but rather, based on Gaddafi's behavior early in the uprising, that such atrocities were likely should the rebels be defeated.

Ten Good Things about Life in Libya under Gaddafi[39]

1. Colonel Muammar Gaddafi considered the home a natural human right.

2. The Libyan government paid for the best education and health care available, including by funding travel abroad for services when necessary.

3. Gaddafi built the world's largest irrigation project, which he personally considered "the eighth wonder of the world."

4. The state provided housing, farmland, livestock, and seeds to any Libyan starting a farming operation.

5. Libya gave the equivalent of USD 5,000 to the mothers of newborns.

6. The government did not charge its citizens for electricity use.

7. Gasoline cost as little as USD 0.14 per liter.

8. Gaddafi increased Libya's literacy rate from 25 percent to 87 percent—with 25 percent of Libyans earning university degrees—during his rule.

9. Libya established its own state bank, which charged 0 percent interest rates and owed no foreign debt.

10. Gaddafi attempted to introduce into world trade a single African currency linked to gold, intended to provide the continent with greater autonomy over its economic affairs.

Barack Obama addressed the nation in a televised speech on March 28, 2011, to announce the imposition of the no-fly zone and, summoning up all his oratorical powers, left no question about his motivations:

Last month, Gaddafi's grip of fear appeared to give way to the promise of freedom. In cities and towns across the country, Libyans took to the streets to claim their basic human rights. As one Libyan said, "For the first time we finally have hope that our nightmare of forty years will soon be over."

Faced with this opposition, Gaddafi began attacking his people . . . . In the face of the world's condemnation, Gaddafi chose to escalate his attacks, launching a military campaign against the Libyan people. Innocent people were targeted for killing. Hospitals and ambulances were attacked. Journalists were arrested, sexually assaulted, and killed. Supplies of food and fuel were choked off. Water for hundreds of thousands of people in Misurata was shut off. Cities and towns were shelled, mosques were destroyed, and apartment buildings reduced to rubble. Military jets and helicopter gunships were unleashed upon people who had no means to defend themselves . . . . Gaddafi declared he would show "no mercy" to his own people. He compared them to rats and threatened to go door to door to inflict punishment. In the past, we have seen him hang civilians in the streets and kill over a thousand people in a single day. Now we saw regime forces on the outskirts of the city. We knew that if we waited—if we waited one more day—Benghazi, a city nearly the size of Charlotte, could suffer a massacre that would have reverberated across the region and stained the conscience of the world . . . . In this particular country— Libya—at this particular moment, we were faced with the prospect of violence on a horrific scale . . . . To brush aside America's responsibility as a leader and—more profoundly—our responsibilities to our fellow human beings under such circumstances would have been a betrayal of who we are. Some nations may be able to turn a blind eye to atrocities in other countries. The United States of America is different. And as president, I refused to wait for the images of slaughter and mass graves before taking action . . . .

I believe that this movement of change cannot be turned back, and that we must stand alongside those who believe in the same core principles that have guided us through many storms: our opposition to violence directed at one's own people; our support for a set of universal rights, including the freedom for people to express themselves and choose their leaders; our support for governments that are ultimately responsive to the aspirations of the people . . . .

It was a stirring address, and it made the humanitarian case quite compellingly. Yet even on its own terms, it gave rise, or should have given rise, to a basic question: Was it true? Was Gaddafi really intent on mass slaughter of his people, or was the administration guilty of, at the very least, gross exaggeration?

Indeed, these noble-sounding words ring especially hollow today, with ISIS spreading terror in the Middle East like no entity ever before. Our opposition to violence directed at one's own people? Our support for a set of universal rights, including the freedom for people to express themselves and choose their leaders? In the face of many times the number of civilian deaths in Iraq and Syria than were ever conceivably at risk in Libya—indeed, with whole populations subject not only to naked brutality, but to ethnic and religious cleansing—the Obama administration long did nothing, and when it finally did act, it was to do very little very late.

Moreover, there now seems no doubt that, in fact, the sensational reports of humanitarian abuses, having been largely generated by Gaddafi's opposition, were vastly overstated.

For obvious reasons, such reports were a source of grave concern to the Gaddafi regime, which rightly viewed them as an existential threat. According to a January 28, 2015, investigative report published in the *Washington Times*, secret audio recordings made at the time of unfiltered conversations between American officials on the ground and Gaddafi's son and heir apparent, Seif, reveal that the younger Gaddafi feared that "Mrs. Clinton was using false pretenses to justify unseating his father and insisted that the regime had no intention of harming a mass of civilians. He compared Mrs. Clinton's campaign for war to that of the George W. Bush administration's now debunked weapons of mass destruction accusations, which were used to lobby Congress to invade Iraq . . . ."

Nonetheless, having made the choice to cast its lot with the "rebels," the Obama administration continued to parrot false claims:

- Throughout the conflict, Western diplomats regurgitated greatly inflated opposition estimates of the death toll,[40] which were then uncritically reported by Western media. Ranging as high as 50,000, these were revealed to be wholly inaccurate in January 2013, when Libya's Ministry of Martyrs and Missing Persons released its official estimate of casualties for the entire war on the rebel side: 4,700 dead combatants and civilians; 2,100 missing. Casualties on the regime's side are thought to be comparable, though no final figure was released.[41]

- Early in the uprising, Western officials repeatedly made the claim that Gaddafi had used armed helicopters to butcher unarmed demonstrators. On February 28, British Prime Minister David Cameron specifically cited this allegation as justification for the no-fly zone. An in-depth report by the International Crisis Group (ICG) later found no evidence that any regime aircraft fired on protestors.[42]

- Allegations of mass rape were an administration favorite, none too subtly playing into Gaddafi's (well-earned) image as a sexual predator. Secretary of State Clinton said that Gaddafi's troops were "using violence against women and rape as tools of war."[43] On April 28, Ambassador Rice told a closed-door meeting of the UN Security Council that Gaddafi was supplying his troops with Viagra to encourage mass rape—a claim that apparently originated with an Al-Jazeera report quoting a local doctor who found the impotency drug in a dead soldier's pockets[44]—as well as deliberately killing children. Many media reports about alleged mass rapes by the Gaddafi regime cited Libyan psychologist Siham Sergewa, who claimed in May 2011 to have interviewed 295 rape victims.[45] However, Sergewa was later unable to provide either documentation or contact information for any alleged victims.[46] Claims of large-scale rape by Gaddafi forces were later debunked by Human Rights Watch,[47] Amnesty International,[48] and the International Crisis Group.[49] UN human rights investigator Cherif Bassiouni, who led a team to Libya in the summer of 2011, likewise could not confirm reports of mass rape, which he suggested were the result of a "massive hysteria."[50]

- American and European officials also publicized reports that Gaddafi was employing thousands of mercenaries from sub-Saharan African countries to kill protestors.[51] Mercenaries "have been turned loose to attack demonstrators," Clinton warned at a February 28 session of the UN Human Rights Council in Geneva.[52]

In fact, rumors of African mercenaries were rooted in the readily observable fact that the rebels had rounded up hundreds of dark-skinned prisoners—scores of whom they executed early in the revolt. Credulous Western journalists accepted the accusations at face value, apparently unaware that Libya has a substantial indigenous minority of sub-Saharan African descent and a sordid history of Arab-on-black racial violence (race riots in October 2000, sparked by a rumor that a Nigerian had raped a Libyan girl, left at least 134 African expatriates and sixteen black Libyans dead).[53] Two weeks into the uprising, one group of rebels actually managed to convince NPR's Lourdes Garcia Navarro that a group of terrified black children in their custody had been airlifted in, given weapons, and sent to fight against the rebels.[54]

Although the myth of African mercenary was debunked by Human Rights Watch in early March[55] (and would be even more definitively debunked by Amnesty International later during the war),[56] NATO officials continued to warn that Gaddafi was attempting to "bring more mercenaries into Libya to defend his regime,"[57] and British Defense Secretary Liam Fox cited the Gaddafi regime's reliance on mercenaries as evidence of how "desperate and weak" it was at an April 26 press conference with his American counterpart.[58]

Although these and other fundamentally bogus charges provided a veneer of credibility to the supposedly humanitarian endeavor, in actuality Obama and his European counterparts were seeking not to bring the killing to a halt or to facilitate a peaceful resolution to the war, but rather to help the losing side win—by definition a pro-longation of the conflict, leading to greater loss of life. Although the White House denied throughout the war that regime change was its goal,[59] regime change was in fact its singular focus. "Our expectation is that as we continue to apply steady pressure, not only militarily but also through these other means, Gaddafi will ultimately step down," Obama conceded during the second week of the campaign.[60]

At least this once, he meant exactly what he said.

5

THE RISE OF LIFG

B ut the most far-reaching deception in the Obama administration's march to war—the classic Big Lie—involved the
role of hardened militant Islamists in the revolt.

With Secretary Clinton leading the way, "tutor[ing] rebels on
the fine points of message management,"[61] the insurgents set up a
National Transitional Council (NTC; also abbreviated TNC) early
on, comprising primarily non-Islamists and nominally led by secularists. Thus NATO's supreme allied commander in Europe, U.S.
Admiral James Stavridis, was able to inform a March 29 Senate
hearing that the rebel leadership was made up of "responsible men
and women" and that there were only "flickers in the intelligence of
potential Al Qaeda."[62] In a June 15 report to Congress justifying the
continued use of force in Libya, the Obama administration stated
flatly, "We have not observed any TNC support or endorsement of
the LIFG."[63] This was an enormous failure of intelligence.

In truth, the NATO military campaign to destroy the Gaddafi
regime was the ideal opportunity for latent jihadist networks to seize
power in many parts of Libya, with the Libyan Islamic Fighting
Group (LIFG) taking a leading role. And, knowingly or not, it was
a task in which the Obama administration was complicit. Driven

by the notion that the jihadists would lay down their weapons and embrace democracy after NATO helped them slay their bête noire, the Obama administration envisaged a scenario in which the broader Arab-Islamic world would see the United States as not being "at war with Islam," with anti-American resentment then fading. Of course, the sheer fantasy of this hope should have been clear from the outset.

In a classic irony, no one better understood the nature of America's "rebel" allies—and the threat that they would ultimately pose to the United States—than Muammar Gaddafi himself. Long before the "Arab Spring" brought on the uprising that loosed massive NATO air power against him, he had battled Libya's home-grown Islamist radicals—had, indeed, battled them with great success. Gaddafi understood full well that they would never become "moderate" or "reasonable"—that their scorn for democracy and individual rights dwarfed even his own.

This is why Gaddafi's long reign had given rise to one of the Arab world's most powerful national jihadist currents in the first place. In a region where even the most secular autocrats pay lip service to core Islamic precepts, Gaddafi forced his overwhelmingly Sunni Muslim subjects to accept sweeping revisions to their creed, including the elimination of the Sunnah (sayings and practices of the Prophet Muhammad) as a source of religious authority and the changing of the Islamic calendar. For devout Sunnis, such apostasy was far worse than professing atheism.

Gaddafi also went much farther than his tyrannical Arab counterparts in eradicating independent religious expression. During the 1970s, his regime heavily suppressed both the Sanusiyya Sufi religious order of ousted King Mohammad Idris and the Libyan chapter of the Muslim Brotherhood (LMB), which saw many of its leaders flee into exile in Europe and the United States. In contrast to the Egyptian branch of the Brotherhood, the LMB was never allowed the opportunity to expand its influence by building a substantial social welfare network.[64]

As a result, fierce animosity between Gaddafi and the Islamists long preceded the rise of global political Islamism. The number of young Libyans drawn to radical Islamism was especially heightened by Gaddafi's deepening relations with the Soviet Union during the 1980s, when the Soviets were at war with Muslim fundamentalists in Afghanistan. Many of those who would later found the radical LIFG were part of an underground circle of Islamist intellectuals centered around future Al Qaeda leader Awad al-Zawawi in the early-to-mid 1980s. Especially prominent in this group was the group's future spiritual leader, Sami al-Saadi (also known as Abu Munthir).

By the early 1990s, the jihadists in Afghanistan included approximately 800 Libyans,[65] who enjoyed a reputation as superior fighters. Operating mostly out of their own camps along the border with Pakistan, the "Libyan Afghans" were rigidly ideological and had a sense of national solidarity unique among Arab fighters.

After Kabul fell to the mujahideen in 1992, a powerful network of Libyan Afghans calling themselves al-Muqatilah (the fighting group) began plotting to carry jihad back to their home country. Many went to Sudan, where Osama bin Laden's emerging Al Qaeda network was establishing a presence, and from there they began secretly infiltrating Libya to set up jihadist cells, planning to slowly put in place a network of operatives before launching overt hostilities against the regime.

But the infiltration did not go unnoticed by Gaddafi's ubiquitous intelligence services. In June 1995, a mission to rescue an injured fighter led to the regime's discovery of a jihadist safe house containing documents that revealed the scale of the infiltration. Not long after, Gaddafi pressured the Sudanese government to expel LIFG members.

In October 1995, after outbreaks of intense anti-regime violence around Benghazi that left dozens dead, representatives of the LIFG in London formally declared the group's existence in a missive calling the overthrow of Gaddafi's "apostate regime" "the foremost duty after faith in God."[66] Soon afterward, led by Abdel-Hakim Belhadj (also known as Abu Abdullah al-Sadeq), who had undergone a baptism by fire fighting against the Soviets, the LIFG began carrying out sporadic attacks on regime targets in northeast Libya. Among these was a February 1996 assassination attempt on Gaddafi that left several of his bodyguards dead.

The regime responded with brutal force, bringing quick success when hundreds of LIFG adherents were rounded up and jailed. Then, in June 1996, in an episode that would be well remembered by vengeful insurgents fifteen years later, Gaddafi's forces killed some 1,200 jihadists in Abu Salim prison, among them two brothers of future "rebel" commander Sami al-Saadi. The "martyrs" of Abu Salim would ever after serve both as an LIFG rallying cry and as an international fundraising tool.

One Libyan operation personally sanctioned by Osama bin Laden—and in association with which he was named, along with three LIFG members, in a 1998 Interpol warrant requested by Gaddafi—was the March 1994 murder of German intelligence officer Silvan Becker and his wife. Among the LIFG coconspirators listed in the warrant was Faraj al-Chalabi (also known as al-Shibli), later identified as a suspect in the planning of the September 11, 2012, attack on the U.S. diplomatic compound in Benghazi.[67]

With the government's crackdown on the group meeting with such stunning success, LIFG leaders deliberated over whether to insinuate the rest of their fighters, scattered around Europe, the Middle East, and Africa, into the battle for Libya, but they narrowly decided against doing so[68]—in part because many LIFG leaders, such as Osama Bin Laden, were ultimately less interested in removing Gaddafi than they were in the larger global jihadist struggle. Although LIFG resistance inside Libya continued, many of the group's leading commanders were pulled out of the country.

A sustained government assault in the summer of 1998 effectively brought what remained of the uprising to a close. Most surviving

LIFG fighters fled to Afghanistan, which had begun welcoming fellow jihadists from throughout the region after the Taliban entered Kabul in 1996. Here, under Belhadj and Saadi, the LIFG built a semi-autonomous network of operatives to fight alongside the Taliban and Al Qaeda. According to one of Belhadj's top associates, he "had a direct line" to bin Laden.

Numerous other LIFG commanders—often distinguishable from others among the welter of names so alien to Western ears by their distinctive "al-Libi" suffix—also assumed leading roles in training Al Qaeda and Taliban fighters for operations against Western targets. Abu al-Laith al-Libi (also known as Ali Ammar Ashur al-Raqiai) was one of Al Qaeda's leading military chiefs until he was killed in Pakistan by a 2008 drone strike. Ibn al-Shaykh al-Libi (also known as Ali Mohamed al-Fakheri) directed the Al-Khaldan training camp near Kabul, which trained at least two of the 9/11 hijackers, 2001 shoe bomber Richard Reid, and many other illustrious jihadist operatives. Abu Anas al-Libi (also known as Nazih Abdul-Hamed Nabih al-Ruqai'i) allegedly planned the 1998 United States embassy bombings in Kenya and Tanzania. Abu Yahya al-Libi (also known as Mohamed Hassan Qaid) was a leading ideologue and propagandist. Abu Faraj al-Libi (also known as Mustafa al-Uzayti) was the third-ranking figure in Al Qaeda until his arrest in 2005 by Pakistani authorities.

At the same time, other LIFG associates found havens in Western countries, particularly Britain—where, as a result of the Lockerbie tragedy, Gaddafi was viewed with particular loathing. Indeed, Britain's MI6 intelligence agency had reportedly aided more than one LIFG attempt on the dictator's life in the 1990s.[69] In Britain, LIFG leaders raised funds, issued press releases, and performed other seemingly legitimate tasks in its continuing agitation against the regime. One LIFG chieftain, Abu Anas al-Libi, lived an outwardly peaceful life in Manchester until May 2000, when police raided his home and discovered 180 pages of detailed jihadist training materials, a gold mine of intelligence subsequently dubbed the "Manchester Manual."[70] It began: "The confrontation we are calling for . . . knows the dialogue of bullets, the ideals of assassination, bombing and destruction, and the diplomacy of the cannon and machine gun." The documents extensively quoted the Qur'an and otherwise provided religious cover for the heinous acts of terrorism, declaring: "The young men returning to Allah realized that Islam is not just performing rituals but a complete system: Religion and government, worship and Jihad, ethics and dealing with people, and the Qur'an and sword. The bitter situation that the nation has reached is a result of its divergence from Allah's course and his righteous law for all places and times."

The shock of September 11, 2001, followed by American military campaigns in Afghanistan and Iraq, cast new light on the role being played by Libyan Islamists in what was at last now widely understood as a worldwide jihadist campaign. Within months of 9/11, the LIFG was declared an Al Qaeda–associated entity by the U.S. government and the UN Security Council. No longer able to travel freely, many of its members did not get very far for very long. Though Belhadj, the emir of LIFG, escaped to Asia for two years, Spanish investigators discovered that he was linked to the horrific March 2004 Madrid train bombings that had left 191 people dead; from China, he had been in phone contact with the attack's ringleader, Serhane bin Abdelmajid Fakhet, as well as with a Jordanian associate of Fakhet.[71] Several weeks after the attack, Belhadj was arrested in Hong Kong and extradited to Libya.

Spiritual leader Sami al-Saadi, linked to a network of Al Qaeda–trained Muslim youths in Britain who had acquired more than half a ton of ammonium nitrate fertilizer they intended for use in car bombing civilian targets, suffered the same fate, being apprehended in Thailand in 2004. He, too, was extradited to Libya.

Similarly, LIFG commanders Khalid al-Sharif (also known as Abu Hazem), Abdul Hakim al-Hasadi, and Abu Sufian bin Qumu (also known as Abdul Faris al-Libi) were arrested by the Pakistanis, handed over to the U.S., and extradited to Libya. All told, at least a dozen leading Libyan jihadists experienced similar involuntary homecomings.

Perhaps because of its enduring hostility to Gaddafi, Britain was slower than its American allies to wholly disavow Gaddafi's Libyan enemies. It was only after the July 2005 London train bombings that the British government designated the LIFG a terrorist group. British police subsequently detained many LIFG figures. Among the most prominent was Abd al-Rahman al-Faqih, an LIFG operative well known to Western intelligence agencies for a range of terrorist-related activities. Found in possession of a CD-ROM labeled "A Special Training Course on the Manufacture of Explosives," Faqih was sentenced to four years in prison.[72] He was later convicted in absentia by the criminal court of appeal of Rabat, Morocco, for involvement in a series of May 2003 suicide bombings in Casablanca that killed at least forty-one people.[73]

By now, LIFG fighters were flocking to Iraq to fight U.S.-led coalition forces. According to a November 2007 examination by the Combating Terrorism Center at West Point of 606 captured personnel files of foreign Al Qaeda operatives in Iraq, Libyans were the second most numerous nationality after Saudis, and by far the most numerous per capita.[74] Astonishingly, the 80,000 inhabitants of Derna, Libya, contributed more jihadists to the Iraq war than did the Saudi capital of Riyadh, a city of 5.2 million.[75] Moreover, even by jihadist standards, the Libyans were unusually committed and hard to break. American interrogators at Guantanamo discovered that they could learn more about LIFG infrastructure in south Asia from non-Libyan jihadists who had trained in it than from the eleven Libyan detainees in their custody.[76]

It hardly went unnoticed—especially by Muammar Gaddafi—that the overwhelming majority of these hardened Libyan fighters came from the country's volatile northeast, particularly from Derna (60 percent) and Benghazi (24 percent). Though at the time his regime was experiencing comparatively little domestic political violence, Gaddafi was keenly aware that conditions in the east were growing ever more conducive to renewed Islamist mobilization. As a 2008 U.S. diplomatic cable later released by WikiLeaks observed, "frustration at the inability of eastern Libyans to effectively challenge Qadhafi's regime" and a "concerted ideological campaign by returned Libyan fighters from earlier conflicts" had produced conditions ripe for jihadist violence.[77]

Moreover, there were signs that Islamists were beginning to gain traction. On February 17, 2006, after a cabinet minister in Rome wore a T-shirt emblazoned with a caricature of the Prophet Muhammad, an infuriated mob set fire to the Italian consulate in Benghazi. The resulting melee between protestors and police left ten dead.[78] Three years later, in May 2009, after the death in prison of LIFG commander Ibn al-Shaykh al-Libi—reportedly by suicide— thousands angrily defied the authorities by attending his funeral.

As always, preoccupied with his own survival—and unquestion- ably made more secure by his newfound sense of solidarity with the West, and especially America—Gaddafi decided that it was time to seek, if only cautiously, to bring his domestic foes into the fold. He was encouraged in this by his second son and heir apparent, Saif al-Islam Gaddafi, a graduate of the London School of Economics— who, though he held no formal government post, wielded consid- erable influence behind the scenes. Much concerned with Libya's appalling human rights record and, hardly incidentally, interested in encouraging tourism, the younger Gaddafi in 2005 launched a reconciliation initiative that offered imprisoned LIFG members and other Islamists amnesty in exchange for renouncing armed opposi- tion to the regime.

Although LIFG leaders in Pakistan and Afghanistan contemp- tuously dismissed any such reconciliation as forced, LIFG leaders in Britain declared their support for it, and many jailed LIFG members accepted the olive branch—or at least gave the appearance of doing so. Signing a 400-page manifesto entitled *Corrective Studies in Understanding Jihad, Accountability, and the Judgment of People*, they renounced rebellion against Muslim rulers and the killing of civilians, offering a formal apology to Gaddafi "for everything we had done against you, starting with the establishment of a secret organization and all the minor and major actions originating from it."[79]

Significantly, for this was a clear sop to the Islamists on the part of the regime, the document allowed that jihad was permitted in Muslim countries that had been "invaded"—specifically, Afghanistan, Iraq, and Palestine[80]—for the reason that "the Jews and Christians" were "enemies" of the worldwide Muslim community "who conquered its lands, plundered its resources and desecrated its sanctities."

Nevertheless, the younger Gaddafi's efforts were appearing to bear fruit. Invited to observe the situation in Libya in 2009, Human Rights Watch reported that observers should not "underestimate the importance of the efforts made so far" by Gaddafi and the regime in curtailing human rights abuses.

Among the scores of leading LIFG figures and veteran operatives released were the group's kingpins, Belhadj and Saadi. The last three years of the Gaddafi regime also witnessed the voluntary repatriation of dozens of Islamists from exile, among them Abu Anas al-Libi, the lead suspect in the 1998 embassy bombings, who had reportedly spent the previous decade in Iran.[81]

Of course, it now hardly needs saying that their avowals of moderation were insincere—that they were only as moderate as they needed to be, and then only very temporarily. Many continued to advocate jihad against U.S. forces in Iraq[82] and to obliquely praise bin Laden.[83] "I don't believe bin Laden is calling for the killing of any single civilian," observed Saadi, managing to keep a straight face. Meanwhile, after leaving prison, others helped recruit Libyans to fight against the United States in Iraq.

If it seems wholly out of character for the canny Gaddafi to have made such a fatal error, it must be borne in mind that at the time it seemed a safe bet. After all, with his domestic jihadist foes seemingly a spent force, surely he could now afford to show them a little magnanimity in the interest of repairing his long-tarnished reputation in the West.

Besides, he was certain he had an ace in the hole—his carefully nurtured friendship with America. This was, after all, an America that, postsurge, appeared to have Iraq under control and Al Qaeda itself on the run. Wasn't it as much in America's interest as in Gaddafi's own to make sure that this remained the case?

Gaddafi was nothing if not a creature of calculation, and the calculation here seemed clear. Surely, he thought, he was safely aligned with the winning side.

6

THE END OF GADDAFI

With images of two seemingly stable neighboring regimes collapsing under the weight of "people power" broadcast around the clock on Al-Jazeera, it is hardly surprising that in early February 2011, Libya, too, began experiencing sporadic anti-government demonstrations.

What is less surprising—and what runs contrary to the mythology peddled by the Obama administration—is that the supposedly "peaceful" demonstrations very quickly turned violent. For although they appeared spontaneous, they were not only well organized, but also purposeful.

The first major confrontation between activists and regime forces took place on February 15, 2011, outside the local security headquarters in Benghazi. It was touched off by the detention of human rights lawyer Fathi Terbil, spokesman for families of those killed in the notorious 1996 Abu Salim massacre. YouTube videos of the event show furious protestors chanting "Muammar is the enemy of Allah" and other Islamist slogans.[84] Although none were killed, several were injured when police (who themselves suffered ten injuries) dispersed the rock-throwing crowd with tear gas and rubber bullets.

Seeking to defuse the rising tide of grievance—in what would arguably be its most fateful mistake—the regime released the last 110 LIFG members still in prison. These included both those who had earlier refused to repent and those deemed for other reasons too dangerous to set free, among them Miftah al-Dhawadi (also known as Abd-al-Ghaffar), the group's first emir; and Mustafa al-Qunayfid (also known as Abu-al-Zubayr), a leading military commander.[85]

In fact, this was a reflection of the American experience with Gitmo: according to some estimates, as many as a third of those released have now returned to terrorist activities—among them Abu Bakr al-Baghdadi, released from Guantanamo in 2009 only to emerge as the leader of ISIS, and for whose recapture the United States was subsequently forced to offer a $10 million reward.[86]

The costs of Gaddafi's release of the jihadists are hard to overstate. Indeed, any faint hope that the supposedly "reformed" Libyan jihadists would calm the waters faded almost immediately when Anis al-Sharif, LIFG's spokesman in London, announced the establishment of a successor organization to continue the anti-Gaddafi struggle, the Libyan Islamic Movement for Change (LIMC).

Though the new LIMC was ostensibly committed to nonviolence, already veteran Islamist operatives inside Libya were moving to seize arms caches. The very day after the group's formation, February 17, police stations and other security offices were torched in the towns of Bayda and Zentan, south of Tripoli.[87] For the Islamists, the February 17 date held particular significance: It was the third anniversary of the burning of the Italian consulate.

Matters escalated quickly. On February 20, a suicide bombing hit the main military barracks in Benghazi, blowing open the gate, enabling rebels to rush the defenders and "liberate" the rest of the city.

By now, longtime LIFG commanders Abu Sufian bin Qumu and Abdul Hakim al-Hasadi were in action, having established a militia force in Derna called the Derna Brigade.[88] On February 23, Hasadi's men ambushed a group of twenty-two soldiers headed for Derna, capturing them all; the next morning, at least a dozen of them were found executed near the village of Makhtuba, east of Derna.[89]

Indeed, the Libyan government was soon claiming, plausibly, that it was Hasadi who was committing atrocities, executing "people who refuse to cooperate with them,"[90] as jihadist forces moved to create an "Islamic emirate." In response, Hasadi declared on Qatar's Al-Jazeera satellite station that he was seeking only the "establishment of a state of justice and liberties."[91]

This was the line adopted by almost all jihadist commanders. The sole major exception was Qumu, who, after escaping from a Libyan prison on drug charges in 1993, had fled to Sudan and fallen in with bin Laden's emerging Al Qaeda network. Following the network to Afghanistan, he was wounded fighting for the Taliban and after 9/11 was arrested by Pakistani police and handed over to the United States. During his incarceration at Gitmo, Qumu was assessed as "likely to pose a threat to the U.S., its interests and allies."[92]

Set free and now operating as a leading rebel commander in his home country, Qumu gave no indication that he had changed in the least. Alone among his colleagues, he refused to so much as speak with Western reporters, once snapping at an intermediary for the *New York Times* to "go to hell" when approached for an interview.[93]

But others in the rebel leadership readily cooperated with a Western press that was seemingly eager to disseminate the administration line. Even longtime LIFG leader Belhadj, who in 1996 had vowed to fight "all the deviant groups that call for democracy or fight for the sake of it," and who had allegedly taken part in the horrific attack on the Spanish trains, now got with the program.

Having taken some months to emerge from hiding, Belhaj spent the early days of the rebellion setting up clandestine cells and safe houses in and around Tripoli before making his way to Benghazi, where he helped organize the February 17 Battalion.[94] But he soon assumed a leadership position, joining other rebel militias for the final assault on the Libyan capital in August as head of the Tripoli Military Council (TMC). In this role, Belhadj assured Western reporters that he favored "a civil country that is ruled by the law" and that "the identity of the country will be left up to the people to choose."[95]

When this declaration aroused the skepticism of certain Spanish reporters, he went out of his way to disavow any role in the railway bombings. Yes, he explained to the Spanish daily *ABC*, bombing ringleader Serhane Bin Abdelmajid Fakhet had indeed phoned him before the attack—but he hadn't picked up, he said, because he hadn't recognized the number. As for his well-publicized call to Fakhet's Jordanian associate, that had been strictly to discuss "personal" matters.[96] So willing were most Westerners to buy Belhaj's claims of newfound moderation that in August, NTC Chairman Mustafa Abdel Jalil felt free to bring him along to an aid conference in Doha, Qatar, where he met with Western diplomats and once again reassured them that he posed "no danger to international peace and stability."[97]

The recent pasts of other Libyan Islamists were likewise regarded as being all but irrelevant. Hasadi openly acknowledged having fought against American forces in Afghanistan before his capture,[98] as well as having sent "about twenty-five" fellow Libyans to fight in Iraq after his release from prison in 2008,[99] but this did not stop him from making brazen demands of his former enemies now. "We need Stingers," Hasadi told one reporter in early March, referring to U.S.-built shoulder-mounted anti-aircraft missiles. "We don't need your stupid words." When reminded that the United States had had great difficulty recovering Stinger missiles supplied to anti-Soviet mujahideen in Afghanistan, he smiled and replied, "This time, we would give them back."[100] After U.S. Deputy Secretary of State James Streingberg was grilled in a March 31, 2011, congressional hearing about Hasadi and other Libyans who had "American blood on their hands,"[101] Hasadi went out of his way to assure the *Wall Street Journal* that "[o]ur view is starting to change of the U.S. If we [previously] hated the Americans 100%, today it is less than 50%. They have started to redeem themselves for their past mistakes by helping us to preserve the blood of our children."[102]

To an administration desperate to believe them, such words fell on receptive ears. During the seven-month campaign targeting pro-Gaddafi forces (or rebel units misidentified as such), NATO forces would fly some 9,700 strike sorties,[103] including those that obliterated the regime's mechanized assault forces on the verge of retaking Benghazi. By war's end, NATO had destroyed more than 600 tanks and armored vehicles, as well as more than 400 artillery and rocket launchers.

Additionally, with the blessing of the Obama administration, Qatar flew an estimated 20,000 tons of weapons to Libya in the spring and summer of 2011. Most of the arms, the *Wall Street Journal* reported, bypassed the National Transitional Council and went "directly to militias run by Islamist leaders."[104] Hundreds of Qatari military personnel entered Libya to train and supervise rebel forces. These advisory teams provided the main link between rebel ground units and NATO's air power.[105] NTC Chairman Jalil later said that Qatar had "planned" the major battles fought by the rebels.[106] The heavy presence of smartly dressed Qatari and UAE special forces in "dune buggy" desert patrol vehicles was evident during the rebel advances on Tripoli in August and on Sirte in October.[107]

In western Libya, the Qataris favored Belhadj, which contributed greatly to the acquiescence of other rebel factions to his leadership. (He reportedly astonished a gathering of militia chiefs by strolling into the meeting accompanied by Qatar's military chief of staff, Major General Hamad Ben Ali al-Attiyah).[108] "This guy is just a creation of the Qataris and their money, and they are sponsoring the element of Muslim extremism here," one TMC member complained to the *New York Times*.[109] In eastern Libya, the Qataris favored Ismail al-Sallabi and others linked to Ali al-Sallabi, who was residing in

Qatar when the revolt broke out and who had grown close to the Qatar-based cleric Yusuf Qaradawi, considered the leading theologian of the international Muslim Brotherhood.

In Benghazi, meanwhile, most rebel recruitment was led by figures affiliated with the LMB. The February 17th Martyrs Brigade, established by Ali al-Sallabi's brother, Ismail, and Fawzi Bukatief, a Muslim Brotherhood member who had spent eighteen years in prison,[110] soon grew into the largest and best-armed militia in the city, with Ismail al-Sallabi named head of the Benghazi Military Council.

Throughout the war, Gaddafi petitioned for ceasefires and dialogue through intermediaries as varied as Turkey, Greece, Malta, the African Union, and UN Secretary-General Ban Ki Moon. "Come France, Italy, UK, America. Come, we will negotiate with you. Why are you attacking us?" Gaddafi pleaded in an April 30, 2011, televised address.[111]

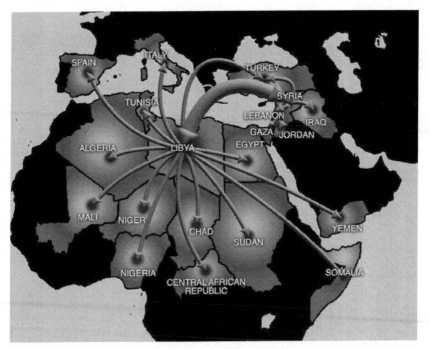

The new spiderweb of the jihadist threat with Libya at its center.
Map: Jason Mintz/IPT

But NATO and the American administration were resolved to continue bombing until "the regime has verifiably withdrawn to bases all military forces, including snipers, mercenaries and other paramilitary forces, including from all populated areas they have forcibly entered, occupied or besieged throughout all of Libya."[112] In other words, until the regime accepted military defeat and loss of power.

By year's end, they got what they wanted—and what followed was entirely predictable. Libya has become a dream come true for the global salafi-jihadist movement. In the shell state that is today's Libya, militant Islamists dominate the quasi-official security forces of what passes for the central government, intimidating secular politicians and killing those they cannot intimidate. Once a logistical and operational dead zone for Al Qaeda, Libya is today a central nexus for training and equipping jihadists across the Middle East, with strategic proximity to Europe.

7

LIBYA:
"SOMALIA ON THE MED"

H ow did post-Gaddafi Libya so quickly arrive at such a calamitous state?

With the longtime dictator's fall, the Obama administration was intent on what it euphemistically called "normalization." As in Afghanistan and Iraq, the aim was to get out as quickly as possible, leaving the lightest possible American footprint, so as never to be mistaken for its predecessor's "green zone" in Baghdad.

More, just as foolishly, the rapid drawdown in Libya reflected the widespread conviction within the administration that American support for the uprising against Gaddafi had already fully secured the enduring gratitude of most Libyans. As Deputy National Security Advisor Denis McDonough put it in May 2012 to a conference at the Washington Institute for Near East Policy, with things already well on the way to falling apart in Libya, "a more democratic region will ultimately be more stable for us and our friends . . . . Even if someone wants to be dictatorial, it's going to be difficult."

This attitude was evident not only in the decision, as in Iraq, to leave no meaningful forces behind to protect America's strategic interests, but also in the decisions made regarding the protection of American diplomatic personnel in the country. Local Libyan contractors and militiamen were hired and trained to guard U.S. diplomats, it being felt that this would be not only less antagonizing to the locals than temporary duty security personnel from out of country, but also more effective. Additionally, the administration believed, it could rely on drone strikes to mitigate security threats—and because the CIA still had wide latitude in Libya, any potential plots directed at American diplomatic posts were sure to be preemptively detected and thwarted.

Obviously, all these guiding assumptions proved false. The light American footprint did nothing to sap Islamist hostilities, which are permanent and intractable. And the modest measures in place to protect diplomats proved woefully inadequate. But of course the gravest error, one of historic proportions, was that of all but ceding the country to the jihadists in the first place.

Not, needless to say, that at the time the president would have acknowledged that that was what NATO was doing. Although at the war's end, the role of Libyan Islamic Fighting Group (LIFG) leaders and other radical Islamists in defeating Gaddafi left them with a commanding armed presence, they by no means enjoyed majority support in the country. To the contrary, Libya's first post-Gaddafi legislative election in 2012 made it clear that outside the eastern Cyrenaica region, home to roughly a third of the population, their support was thin. Nationwide, Mahmoud Jibril's secularist National Forces Alliance (NFA)[113] won the largest bloc of seats in the newly constituted legislature, with 48 percent of the vote. Indeed, this emboldened the Obama administration to briefly claim Libya a success story: Here was a Muslim nation long under the heel of a ruthless tyrant that was now—thanks to America—emerging as a democracy.

If such a view reflected the usual degree of wishful thinking and willful blindness, the election results simultaneously confirmed the

LIBYA: "SOMALIA ON THE MED"

jihadist conviction that the surest route to an Islamic Libya—one that in the interim would serve as a vast terrorist training ground— was a Libya so chaotic that it would no longer be a functioning state at all.

This was the gift the feckless Obama administration policy readily granted them.

If there remained the slightest doubt whether their collective "moderation" had ever been more than a pose, it quickly vanished. Not only did the jihadists fail to surrender their weapons with Gaddafi's fall, but many quickly left for the next major front in the global jihadist struggle: Syria.

Meanwhile, those who stayed continued the fight, if sometimes by other means. A number of key rebel commanders traded in their fatigues for tailored suits and entered politics, perverting the system from within. Others integrated themselves into the quasi-official postwar security infrastructure. Still others forged new jihadist networks aimed at undermining civil society by targeting democratic and Western interests and imposing *sharia*.

This was entirely consistent with the LIFG's pre-revolt *modus operandi*, whereby the group's various arms performed different but complementary functions. In the new Libya, the Islamists in the security services ensured that local terrorists were able to operate with impunity even as they prevented democratically elected secular leaders from exerting meaningful authority.

Crucially, the new reality allowed for the easy redistribution of weapons—both those that had been provided by the West and the caches seized from the old regime—to new fronts in the Islamic struggle. Of particular value was Gaddafi's vast store of shoulder-fired missiles (MANPADS). Notwithstanding Secretary Clinton's assurance that America was "helping Libya secure and destroy dangerous stockpiles of weapons," vast caches of MANPADS were funneled to jihadists in Syria.

Unsurprisingly, the administration kept the ineffectual weapons securement program, especially the efforts to buy back the MANPADS, shrouded in mystery. In March 2013, a "well-placed source" reported to CBS News's Sharyl Attkisson that the anti-proliferation team "offered them [Libyan militiamen] money."[114] However, in April, State Department spokeswoman Nicole Thompson told investigative journalist Marinka Peschmann that the State Department "does not operate any weapons 'buy-back' or acquisition programs in Libya," which suggested that State's attempt to retrieve the weapons had been something other than a resounding success. According to unidentified U.S. officials cited by Reuters, the CIA base in Benghazi was merely "collecting information" on the proliferation of weapons looted from Gaddafi's arsenals. In any case, by the time of the September 2012 attack, at least several thousand MANPADS remained unrecovered.

The United States and other Western governments paid even less attention to the fate of other conventional weapons that had been given to or captured by the Libyan militias. "We were raising the alarm bell with the U.S. government, and they were very interested in talking to us about the missing surface-to-air-missiles," said Peter Bouckaert, emergencies director at Human Rights Watch, "but they were singularly uninterested in what would happen with the more run-of-the-mill weapons." The reason, he suggests, is that only the MANPADS had the potential to be politically embarrassing for the American and British governments. "The MANPADS were a very serious matter, and you can imagine what a nightmare it would have been for the U.S. or UK if one of their civilian planes was shot down by a MANPAD that had gone missing in Libya when they supported the opposition."

While a supposed humanitarian relief organization called the Libyan Council for Relief and Support set up collection centers for gathering and redistributing arms abroad, the Libyan government, such as it was, looked the other way. "We don't stop them, because we know what the Syrian people are going through," the Libyan government official responsible for letting the shipments leave Benghazi explained to Reuters. In its final report on Benghazi, the House Permanent Select Committee on Intelligence stated that the "CIA was collecting intelligence about foreign entities that were themselves collecting weapons in Libya and facilitating their passage to Syria." Although the report does not address whether any U.S. government agencies or contractors might have been involved in this process, what the United States was in fact doing in Benghazi is a question that to date has never been answered—but weapons shipments are near the core of the story.

Gang of Eight — the people who would've known what was going in Benghazi...

Legislation enacted in 1980 provided the executive branch with the authority to limit advance notification of especially sensitive covert actions to eight members of Congress—known as the "Gang of Eight"—when the president determines that limiting prior notice is essential to meeting extraordinary circumstances affecting vital U.S. interests.

In such cases, the executive branch is permitted by statute to limit notification to the chairmen and ranking minority members of the two congressional intelligence committees, the speaker and minority leader of the House, and the Senate majority and minority leaders. The executive is not required to notify the full intelligence committees as is required in cases involving covert actions that are determined to be less sensitive.

Congress approved the Gang of Eight procedure in 1980 during the Iran hostage crisis and narrowed its scope in 1991, after the Iran–Contra Affair.[115]

At the same time, the Libyan jihadists were focused on the African nations to the south, whose unstable governments, ethnic divisions, and feeble defenses left them especially vulnerable to Islamist exploitation—a major reason why many of those governments had supported Gaddafi during the war. One early target was Mali. Both Algeria and Niger soon became conduits for Libyan arms into Mali, with multiple shipments intercepted. In February 2012, Algerian authorities seized fifteen SA-24 and twenty-eight SA-7 MANPADS at a location near Amenas; in October 2013, Algeria seized a huge cache of Mali-bound arms, including more than 500 MANPADS, near its border with Libya. During 2011–2012, the Tunisian military also intercepted numerous weapons in transit from Libya.

In March 2012, Al Qaeda affiliate Ansar Dine seized control of Timbuktu and other major northern Mali towns and began enforcing *sharia* there. It was later joined by the Movement for Oneness and Jihad in West Africa (MOJWA), a splinter group of Al Qaeda in the Islamic Maghreb (AQIM), and by Mokhtar Belmokhtar's forces.

In May 2013, Niger foreign minister Mohamed Bazoum warned that jihadists driven out of northern Mali by the French-led intervention forces had found shelter in southwest Libya, noting that Libya as a whole "is one of the biggest international terrorism bases." Three weeks later, twin suicide bombs in Niger killed twenty-four soldiers, with Belmokhtar claiming responsibility.

Officials in Nigeria, where the jihadist organizations Boko Haram and Ansaru have waged a bloody insurgency since 2009, likewise say that the level of violence has spiked markedly owing to the influx of Libyan weapons and the battlefield experience gained by Nigerian jihadists fighting in Mali. And Chad's ministry of defense said in June 2012 that thirty MANPADS from Libya were bought from Tebu traffickers, with the country's president claiming in April 2013 that Benghazi was now home to training camps for Chadian rebel fighters.

In April 2013, a UN Security Council Panel of Experts issued a report citing evidence of illicit arms transfers from Libya to more than a dozen countries in Africa and the Levant, where the weapons are "fuelling existing conflicts . . . and enriching the arsenals of a range of non-state actors, including terrorist groups." Less than a year later, in February 2014, the same UN panel reported that it had "documented transfers of Libyan MANPADS and other short range surface to air missiles in four different countries: including Chad, Mali, Tunisia, Lebanon and potentially in the Central African Republic."

Nor has neighboring Egypt been immune to the malign influence of Libyan Islamists. The flow of Libyan weapons into Egypt has been substantial and difficult to stanch owing to the two countries' long shared border. Most of the weapons end up in Sinai, where jihadist groups have grown steadily stronger, and Gaza, where the militant Palestinian Islamist Hamas movement reigns supreme. According to the U.S. State Department, the Muhammad Jamal Network (MJN), an Egyptian group closely affiliated with Al Qaeda and AQIM, has established at least one training camp in eastern Libya. In February 2014, former Egyptian deputy chief of staff Major General Mohamed Ali Bilal warned that Libya "has become the hotbed to prepare for invading Egypt." According to Bilal, many of the terrorists operating in Sinai were smuggled in from Libya.

At the same time, the chaos within Libya allowed for the creation of terrorist training camps, among them those explicitly intended for Islamists recruited from other countries, including those in the West. Indeed, a joint 2012 investigation by Algerian and French security services examining the cases of twenty-one Algerians and five French citizens who had fought with jihadists in Syria found that every one had passed through Libya. Although most of the Muslim youth who come to train in Libya may initially do so with the intention of fighting in Syria, they are often diverted to other fronts in the global jihad after being trained.

Although Americans—at least those who care to know—are well versed in what happened in Benghazi on September 11, 2012, many of the other consequences of Gaddafi's fall and of the Obama administration's subsequent abandonment of the country have received almost no coverage. How many are aware, for example, that Islamic terrorists almost surely got their hands on the remnants of Gaddafi's chemical weapons arsenal of sulfur mustard gas, only about half of which had been destroyed at the time of the uprising? The tragedy of misbegotten American policy in Libya continues to unfold, and only the most deluded optimists believe that there will not be more bad news to come.

If you break it, as the saying goes, you own it. As former Secretary of State Colin Powell famously noted, in regard to Iraq, "once you bring down a government, you become the government," and "we made serious mistakes in not acting like a government. One, maintaining order. Two, keeping people from destroying their own property. Three, not having in place security forces—either ours or theirs or a combination of the two to keep order. And *in the absence of order, chaos ensues* [emphasis mine]."[116]

8

THE MILITIAS UNLEASHED

Although Libya's transitional government nominally brought the Islamist militias under its control by absorbing them into organizations theoretically answerable to the army chief of staff and the interior ministry—the wholesomely named Libya Shield and the Supreme Security Committees—in fact they remained in the hands of their previous commanders.

Operating in east and central Libya, Libya Shield was drawn mainly from the February 17th Martyrs Brigade and other Muslim Brotherhood–affiliated militias. Its most prominent commander was Wisam bin Hamid, a reputed Iraq war veteran[117] and militant Islamist,[118] and under his direction, any pretense that the group was interested in order or evenhandedness soon vanished. Deployed in April 2012 to the Kufra district to halt clashes between Arab militias and the minority Tebu tribe, Libya Shield actually joined the assault on the Tebu, which accused them of pursuing "an extermination policy." Similarly, Coptic Christians in Benghazi accused the Martyr Rafallah Sahati Brigade, newly absorbed into Libya Shield, of targeting them. Unbound by any governmental authority whatsoever, militiamen affiliated with Libya Shield and the Supreme Security Committees in May 2013 went so far as to besiege the parliament and several government ministries, demanding that lawmakers pass a ban forbidding Gaddafi-era officials in government service—an extraordinary blow to secular politicians. They got their way.

Other Islamist militias were also openly engaged in targeting domestic enemies and otherwise wreaking havoc. For instance, the Nawasi brigade, an Islamist militia in Tripoli led by Abdel-Raouf Al-Karah, destroyed an historic Sufi mosque and became known for rounding up homosexuals and others accused of "deviant" behavior.[119] During one particularly destructive weekend in August 2012, Islamists blew up the tomb of fifteenth-century Sufi scholar Abdel Salam al-Asmar, a nearby library, and a mosque housing the shrine of Sufi mystic Sidi Shaab in the Libyan city of Zlitan. Security forces stationed nearby did nothing to intervene; as it turned out, some of the attackers were themselves members of the Supreme Security Committee. Indeed, by the summer of 2012, Libya was witnessing widespread destruction and vandalism of Sufi shrines and mosques;[120] as well as desecrations of British World War II graves, small-scale attacks on foreign consulates, and a campaign of assassinations and kidnappings of former Gaddafi regime officials and other secularists.[121] In 2012, eighteen senior security officials, as well as at least twenty others, were murdered.[122] According to *Jane's Intelligence Review*, there were eighty-three such assassinations (of 135 attempts) in 2013, many of them of secular judges, activists, and others who had no connection to Gaddafi—including moderate imams who had condemned previous killings.[123]

The refusal of the Islamist militias to submit to governmental authority led to frequent civilian protests calling for their disarmament,[124] which in turn resulted in violent reprisals by the militias. In January 2013, they opened fire on protesters in Tripoli, leaving five dead.[125] Five months later, Libya Shield fighters fired on protesters swarming their Benghazi headquarters, killing at least twenty-seven.[126] No one was ever charged for the crime.

Among the reconstituted postwar Libyan jihadist groups, the largest—and the one with which many Americans would eventually become most familiar—was Ansar al-Sharia ("partisans of Islamic law") in Benghazi (ASB), founded shortly after the end of the civil war by Muhammad al-Zahawi and unveiled publicly in February 2012. An affiliated Ansar al-Sharia chapter was later founded in Derna (ASD). Both would be involved in the September 2012 attack on the American diplomatic mission in Benghazi.

Longtime LIFG chief Abdel-Hakim Belhadj, who in the past had openly expressed his contempt for democratic processes, was among the jihadist leaders who took the political path, founding the al-Watan party; his longtime associates Saadi and Qaid formed the even more rigidly Islamist Umma al-Wasat party. Although Belhadj's messaging was now studiously refined,[127] it was often framed with emphatic warnings both to the West and to secular Libyans.

The threats were not idle: The supposedly reformed LIFG emir remained plugged into Al Qaeda's affiliates in north Africa and has since been linked to the 2013 assassinations of secular liberal Tunisian activists Chokri Belaid and Mohammed Brahmi. Indeed, the representative of the Tunisian nongovernmental commission charged to investigate the killings reported that at least three members of the cell responsible for the killings had been trained by Belhadj.[128] Algerian officials agreed, with a senior official quoted in Echorouke Online saying, "This Libyan man is known for his armed actions in Afghanistan and Libya. He funded the group which carried out many attacks and murders." Consequently, Belhadj is not allowed to enter Algeria.

Nonetheless, in their guise as legitimate politicians, Belhadj and other jihadists were positioned to place fellow Islamists in key positions in the Libyan government and security apparatus. Former LIFG commander Khalid al-Sharif organized some 10,000 militiamen into the official-sounding "National Guard," supposedly charged with providing border security and guarding high value former regime officials. His LIFG compatriot Abd al-Wahhab Qaid was appointed commander of the border guards in southern Libya.[129] Former LIFG leader Sadiq al-Ghaithi (also known as Sadiq al-Obeidi) served as deputy defense minister, and another former LIFG member and admitted Iraq war recruiter,[130] Ibrahim al-Jathran, was named commander of the Petroleum Facilities Guard (PFG), a 30,000-strong unit charged with protecting oil installations in Libya.[131] Former LIFG emir Miftah al-Dhawadi was appointed deputy minister of martyrs and missing persons in the government of Interim Prime Minister Abdul Rahim al-Keib.[132] Former LIFG London spokesman Anis al-Sharif was appointed operations manager of Al-Naba TV, a Qatari-funded channel that *Maghreb Confidential* calls "a local Al-Jazeera clone," in 2013.[133]

Although these and many others were chiefly concerned with marginalizing and eliminating political opposition, the Islamists never lost sight of their jihadist mission. As early as October 2011, even ostensibly secularist leaders, were kowtowing to the militias' diktats, fearful of their unchecked power, with NTC Chairman Jalil, nominally a secularist, declaring that *sharia* would now be the principal source of law in the new Libya. "Any law that violates *sharia*," he proclaimed, "is null and void legally"—adding that the Gaddafi-era law restricting polygamy "is contrary to *sharia* and it is stopped."[134] For the same reason, he said, interest on loans "will be ruled out."[135]

The Islamist Libyan Transitional Council had named Tripoli-based scholar and author Sheikh Sadeq al-Ghariani its grand mufti—the highest-ranking official on Islamic law in Muslim countries—as the civil war to depose Colonel Muammar Gaddafi raged in 2011.[136] Al-Ghariani issued postwar fatwas that few dared defy. Typical was the one requiring female teachers to veil if they had male students above the age of puberty.[137]

With the imposition of *sharia*, the wholesale abandonment of democratic norms became all too clear, and some in Europe began voicing their concern. "This is a problem for us," declared French

Foreign Minister Alain Juppe, "especially in regard to respect for the dignity of women."

Al-Ghariani reinstated Libya's office for religious edicts, Dar Al-Ifta, which Gaddafi had abolished during his reign. He also declared that *sharia* law would serve as the primary source of legislation and that any law contradicting Islam was invalid.[138] He legitimized polygamy,[139] as well as issuing fatwas against a UN report on violence against women[140] and banning Libyan women from marrying foreigners.[141] He also called on the ministry of education to delete passages on democracy and freedom of religion from school textbooks.[142] He praised the militant group Ansar al-Sharia, which the United States blames for killing U.S. Ambassador Christopher Stevens and three other Americans in Benghazi on September 11, 2012.[143] In August 2014, the British government accused al-Ghariani of also using a UK-based Internet TV channel to encourage Islamist fighters with ideological ties to ISIS to overthrow the Libyan parliament.[144]

But whatever leverage the NATO powers might have had over events in Libya had disappeared with their heedless withdrawal; and in any case, the reaction from the country most responsible for the intervention on the "rebels'" behalf was muted. Even now, the Obama administration scarcely seemed to understand the Islamists' true nature or that their ultimate aim was not merely to impose their horrific views in their own country, but also to export jihad throughout the region and the world.

9

BENGHAZI AND THE MOUNTING COSTS OF REMOVING GADDAFI

The September 11, 2012, assaults on the U.S. diplomatic mission and CIA annex in Benghazi would have represented a dark day for the United States even had everyone escaped alive, for the accompanying loss of the intelligence assets was itself a catastrophe of massive proportions. Those assets had enabled American operatives to attempt to track the terrorist threat that had been growing ever more ominous since the fall of Libya to Islamic militants. Although how effective those efforts were remains a point of contention—the intelligence community picked up no actionable intelligence about the impending attacks—what is certain is that whatever capabilities there had been were now gone. America was now left essentially blind, deaf, and dumb. And the terrorists knew it.

Characteristically, though, the administration's instinct was to fudge, to obfuscate, and to outright lie. American officials referred to the CIA operatives who had broken cover, leaving their compound to rescue survivors of the initial attack on the mission, as a "quick reaction force" dedicated to diplomatic security. Of course, this was by no means their intended function, and saving those who managed to escape the burning compound came at a heavy cost: Afterward, the jihadists were able to track CIA vehicles returning to the annex from the compound or carrying newly arrived Tripoli agents from the airport to the annex. Two more Americans died there, and the jihadists soon overran the CIA's largest station in North Africa. The documents they found almost surely soon made their way to "core" Al Qaeda leadership in south Asia.[145]

What remains astonishing even now is how utterly avoidable this calamity was. How could it have happened? How could so little security have been provided for American personnel left smack dab in the middle of the region's most lawless, extremist-plagued city?

After all, by then the warning signs were everywhere. Islamist attacks on Western targets in Benghazi were occurring regularly, and even the International Committee of the Red Cross (ICRC) had pulled out of the city. Little wonder that Ambassador Chris Stevens and others on the ground in Libya had repeatedly urged their superiors to deploy more security personnel. Instead, they got fewer—and were told to stop asking.[146]

Nor, as senior White House and State Department officials afterward maintained, was this a merely a tragic blunder, or a mid-level leadership failure, or bureaucratic mismanagement, or anything else reflecting the routine malfunctioning of unwieldy government agencies. On their own authority, mid-level bureaucrats do not reduce the number of American security personnel at a weakly defended diplomatic post facing growing security threats.

But if this was madness, there was method to it.

Though Secretary of State Clinton would later claim that she had been wholly out of the loop, seeking to attribute the disaster to "imperfect information" imparted by subordinates,[146] unclassified diplomatic cables, memos, and congressional testimony suggest that she herself approved the drawdown of U.S. security personnel—not because she failed to recognize the threat to American lives posed by ascendant jihadist forces, but because the administration continued to believe that the best way of minimizing such threats was to shrink the size of the American footprint. To do otherwise, they thought, would have the opposite effect, making American personnel more likely to be targeted. In any case, they had persuaded themselves, the Islamists remained deeply grateful for the role America had played in easing them to power.

So how did those we had counted on for their loyalty react that night? The "trusted" Libyan police units stationed along checkpoints leading to the mission made no attempt to block the attackers from approaching, and both the militiamen assigned to defend the facility and the local contractors charged to sound the alarm cut and ran—or joined in the assault.

If there is one thing we can assume with certainty about Ambassador Stevens, he, unlike his superiors, should have known exactly with whom, and with what, he was dealing. An experienced Arabic-speaking diplomat who had earlier served as deputy chief of mission in Libya and who personally knew some of the regime defectors who had nominally led the rebellion,[147] Stevens had been a natural fit for the job of U.S. Special Representative to the NTC during the early weeks of the war. Although in a 2008 diplomatic cable he had described Gaddafi as an "engaging and charming interlocutor" and a "strong partner in the war against terrorism,"[148] after the uprising began, Stevens was on board with administration policy, now a staunch advocate of American military intervention against the Libyan dictator. According to *New York Times* journalist David D. Kirkpatrick, he had "helped shape the Obama administration's conviction that it could work with the rebels," even those previously hostile to the West, to build a friendly, democratic government.[149]

After arriving in Benghazi aboard a Greek cargo ship in April 2011, Stevens's eight-man team was in daily contact for seven months with the rebel leadership on matters ranging from military strategy to municipal services, coordinating the delivery of American (nonlethal) military and humanitarian assistance. The delegation stayed in a hotel until a bomb exploded in the parking lot in June. After relocating briefly to the CIA annex, the team settled in one of the many gated villa compounds that dot the posh Fwayhat district of western Benghazi. Then known as the U.S. liaison office, this was the only American diplomatic outpost in Libya after the closure of the American embassy in Tripoli and the departure of Ambassador Gene Cretz at the end of February 2011. Stevens was dubbed by his colleagues "the expeditionary diplomat."[150]

With the fall of Tripoli to the rebels, the American embassy was reopened, and most U.S. diplomatic personnel were relocated to the Libyan capital. This left the United States with two posts in Benghazi—the rump liaison office, now called the Temporary Mission Facility (TMF), and the burgeoning CIA installation that would come to be known as "the annex."

By mid-2012, the TMF had largely dropped off the map as a diplomatic outpost. Aside from one flurry of reports about a June 2012 IED attack on the outer walls of the American "consulate" in Benghazi, the first nine months of the year saw almost no Western media mention of any U.S. diplomatic presence in Benghazi. Nor should there have been. According to the December 2012 report of the Accountability Review Board (ARB) charged by Secretary of State Clinton to investigate the Benghazi attacks, the TMF "was never a consulate," but rather "a temporary, residential facility, not officially notified to the host government."[151] It was staffed entirely by temporary duty diplomatic personnel who usually served for a few months or less, very often without transiting through Tripoli. In part, this was because the assignment was so unattractive—diplomats stationed there spent the vast majority of their time holed up inside the compound.

Security was minimal, consisting of three Diplomatic Security (DS) agents inside the compound, along with a handful of unarmed local contractors—charged to screen visitors, sound the alarm, and perform other nonlethal tasks—and a four-man team outside the gate, provided by the February 17th Martyrs Brigade.

After returning to Libya in May 2012, after stateside consultations, Stevens, newly installed as ambassador to replace Cretz, conspicuously went the entire spring and summer without visiting Benghazi, which had become increasingly lawless and violent since the end of the war. Black flags proliferated as Islamist militias abandoned the wartime pretenses that had been needed to draw Western support. The place was returning to its roots.

The continued existence of the TMF was something of a compromise. Senior State Department officials felt that some form of diplomatic presence in Benghazi was critical, largely to reassure the many influential figures based in the city that the interests of eastern Libyans would not be neglected.[152] And indeed, noted Assistant Secretary for Near Eastern Affairs Jeffrey Feltman in December 2011 after a visit to the city, many Libyans said that the U.S. presence in Benghazi had "a salutary, calming effect on easterners who are fearful that the new focus on Tripoli could once again lead to their neglect and exclusion from reconstruction and wealth distribution and [who] strongly favor a permanent U.S. presence in the form of a full consulate." It was precisely for this reason that most Western governments had maintained permanent diplomatic posts in Benghazi during the Gaddafi regime.

Although the TMF was largely symbolic, the CIA annex a mile away was extremely active, the agency having recognized, almost immediately after the city fell to the rebels at the start of the war in February 2011, the need to establish a presence in Benghazi. Tasked by the administration with providing various kinds of assistance to the rebel coalition, the CIA compound quickly became the agency's largest facility in north Africa.

Though described by Obama administration officials as an "annex" or "safe house" for diplomatic personnel in the days after the September 11, 2012, attack,[153] the CIA compound was nothing of the sort. On the contrary, the so-called "annex" operated independently of the TMF and had a far more vital purpose. The fact is, the TMF functioned more as an adjunct of the CIA station, providing diplomatic cover to many of its operatives rather than the other way around. Of the more than thirty U.S. personnel evacuated from Benghazi, only seven actually worked for the State Department.[154] Both former Navy SEALs killed in the Benghazi attack—Tyrone Woods and Glen Doherty—were contracted by the CIA.[155]

For obvious reasons, the CIA went to a great deal of trouble to keep the annex and its activities under wraps locally—a state of affairs it felt necessary to maintain even after the attack. Slow to publicly acknowledge that Wood and Doherty were operatives, the agency's director at the time, David Petraeus, did not attend their funerals.[156]

Libyan Deputy Prime Minister Mustafa Abushagour later told the *Wall Street Journal* that he had learned about the extent of American intelligence operations in Benghazi only in the aftermath of the attack on the mission, when more than two dozen U.S. personnel were evacuated from the city's airport.[157] On the day after the attack, the CIA apparently dispatched Libyan agents to destroy sensitive equipment and documents.[158]

Even within the government, the existence of the annex was a closely guarded secret. According to a January 2014 report by the Senate Select Committee on Intelligence (SSCI), the command of U.S. AFRICOM was not made aware of a CIA facility in Benghazi,[159] even though it might well have been called upon to plan a rescue of U.S. personnel from the city.

Officially, the annex was primarily involved in surveillance of Islamist militants and in helping State Department contractors and Libyan officials track MANPADS seized by militias during the war. However, there have been numerous unconfirmed reports of the annex's having served other purposes. In November 2011, Fox News cited "multiple intelligence sources who have served in Benghazi" as saying that several prisoners were being held at the CIA annex, including both Libyan militiamen and terror suspects from other countries brought to the compound for interrogation.[160] There has also been much speculation that the CIA annex in Benghazi was involved in facilitating the shipment of arms from Libya to Syria. By June 2012, CIA officers in Turkey and the region at large were helping coordinate arms distribution to Syrian rebels, vetting the recipients.[161]

In any case, it is clear that even after the attack, the CIA was intent on keeping the particulars of its activity within the annex a secret. Indeed, in January 2013, four months after the attack, the agency reportedly began subjecting personnel who had served in Benghazi to lie detectors to determine whether any had been speaking to the media. For the record, a CIA spokesman denied that the employees had been subjected to "any non-routine security procedures."[162]

Stevens's decision to return to Benghazi in October was prompted by his growing—and well-founded—concern about security threats in the city. Against a backdrop of rampant political violence, assassinations, and a near absence of government authority, jihadist attacks on American and Western targets in the city, as well as more mundane security incidents, were being regularly detailed in memos[163] dispatched to Washington by Regional Security Officer (RSO) Eric Nordstrom. In all, Nordstrom listed more than 200 security threats and violent incidents between June 2011 and July 2012, at least fifty of them in Benghazi. Among the most notable were the following:[164]

Violent Incidents in Benghazi

March 18	An armed robbery takes place at the British School in Benghazi.
March 22	A suspect demands entry into the TMF while kicking the entry gate. "The local guard on duty fled the gate area," says Nordstrom's memo.
April 2	A British diplomatic vehicle is damaged by attackers after it drives through a local demonstration.
April 6	An IED is thrown over the north wall of the TMF by two Libyan former contractors for the TMF.
April 10	An attacker throws an IED at a convoy in Benghazi carrying the head of the UN mission in Libya.
May-August	Five attacks take place against International Committee of the Red Cross (ICRC) facilities in Benghazi and Misrata. The previously unknown Brigades of the Imprisoned Sheikh Omar Abdul Rahman claim responsibility, accusing the ICRC (which uses a red cross as an emblem) of distributing Bibles and engaging in other proselytizing activities.
June 6	An IED attack blows a 9- by 12-foot hole in the perimeter wall of the TMF. The Omar Abdul Rahman group claims responsibility for what it calls an assault on "Christian overseers" preparing to receive one of the "heads of instigation" from the State Department, a possible reference to Stevens's subsequently aborted plans to visit Benghazi that month.
June 11	An RPG attack on the British ambassador's convoy wounds two security guards.

Nordstrom's appeals for more security were technically only recommendations, because Deputy Assistant Secretary for Diplomatic Security Charlene Lamb discouraged Nordstrom and Stevens from filing formal requests for security. They thus elicited no cable response, nor have documents come to light showing that he formally rejected them. Deputy Assistant Secretary Lamb later testified before the House Oversight Committee in October that "we had the correct number of assets in Benghazi at the time of 9/11 for what had been agreed upon."[165] Nonetheless, senior officials in Washington were indisputably aware of the dangers facing American personnel in Benghazi.

Indeed, even as Assistant Secretary Lamb emphatically discouraged Stevens and Nordstrom from making security requests, she struck a different tone in emails with her superiors. In a June 11 email exchange with Scott Bultrowicz, she wrote: "This is very concerning when you start putting the events together: The recent big demonstration that was openly anti-American, the attack on our compound, and now this UK motorcade attack. If the tide is turning and they are now looking for Americans and Westerners to attack that is a game changer. We are not staffed or resourced adequately to protect our people in that type of environment. We are a soft target against the resources available to the bad guys there."[166]

Little wonder that in summer 2012, department personnel serving in Benghazi reportedly received an increase in their hardship and danger pay allowance to 30 percent of base pay,[167] or that in August, the department issued a travel warning for U.S. citizens in Libya,[168] citing the recent spree of assassinations and car bombings.

In addition to an enormous volume of threat reporting from the Libya embassy, American intelligence agencies produced "hundreds of analytic reports in the months preceding the September 11–12, 2012, attacks," according to the January 2014 SSCI report, "providing strategic warning that militias and terrorist and affiliated groups had the capability and intent to strike U.S. and Western facilities and personnel in Libya."[169] Several of these reports specifically predicted future attacks:

- A June 2012 report by the Defense Intelligence Agency (DIA), "Libya: Terrorists Now Targeting U.S. and Western Interests," predicted "more anti-U.S. terrorist attacks in eastern Libya."[170]

- On June 18, 2012, the daily intelligence report of the Pentagon's Joint Staff included a slide headlined "Terrorism: Conditions Ripe for More Attacks, Terrorist Safe Haven in Libya," warning of growth in "Libyan terrorist capability in the permissive post-revolution security environment" and predicting that "attacks will also increase in number and lethality as terrorists connect with AQ associates in Libya" and that "areas of eastern Libya will become a safe haven by the end of 2012."[171]

- An August 19 report of the Joint Staff predicted that "conditions in Libya will allow terrorists to increase attacks against Western and Libyan interests in the country, as well as [to] attempt attacks in the region and possibly Europe in the next six months."[172]

Hardly incidentally, the growing jihadist threat led other international actors and other parts of the U.S. government to either upgrade their security posture in Benghazi or leave the city entirely. The British closed their Benghazi mission a day after the assault on their ambassador. The ICRC evacuated Benghazi and Misrata in August. After that, the UN also suspended its presence. As RSO Nordstrom later recalled, "[I]t was apparent to me that we were the last flag flying in Benghazi. We were the last thing on their target list to remove from Benghazi."[173]

Yet in spite of the June IED attack on the TMF (and even as the CIA extensively upgraded its security at the annex),[174] no material changes were made at the compound. The State Department was determined to stay in Benghazi but also maintain its current minimal security posture. And this was not for want of continued efforts on the part of those closest to the situation, who continued to request— and be denied—additional security assets.

The question is: Why? Why were multiple requests for the added security that was so obviously essential repeatedly rejected? It appears that the main reason was the State Department's and Secretary Clinton's single-minded obsession with "normalizing" its footprint in Libya, which meant depending less on armed U.S. agents and soldiers to defend American personnel and more on locals.

"I first saw that term, 'normalization,' in that budget proposal, resource proposal, a month after we had arrived," RSO Nordstrom testified in May 2013. ". . . It struck me as being part of some sort of script, just like the reason we didn't close the facility in Benghazi despite the risks. There was already a political decision that said, we're going to keep that."[175]

Astonishingly, on the night of the attack, the TMF wouldn't even have the full complement of five DS agents allocated by Under Secretary of State for Management Patrick F. Kennedy in a December 2011 memorandum.[176] Indeed, the ARB report later found that a full complement of five DS agents had been deployed at the mission for a mere twenty-three days in 2012, with the number most of the time dropping to three—and sometimes to as low as one.[177]

Why did Ambassador Stevens return to Benghazi when he knew that the security situation in the city was so uncertain, let alone on the anniversary of the 9/11 terror attacks? Former deputy chief of mission in Libya Gregory Hicks later testified before a congressional committee that Stevens told him that it was because "Secretary Clinton wanted Benghazi converted into a permanent constituent post" and needed him "to report before September 30th, the end of the fiscal year, on the physical and the political and security environment in Benghazi to support an action memo to convert Benghazi from a temporary facility to a permanent facility."[178]

On September 10, his first day back in Benghazi, the ambassador met with the mayor and twenty local council members at the El Fadeel Hotel. That night, he attended a dinner party with "Adel Jalu," whom he describes as an "hotelier and caterer extraordinaire," and whom he appears to have known from his previous stay in the city. Afterward he wrote in his diary that the guests exchanged "some heated words" about the Muslim Brotherhood.[179]

The following day, September 11, the ambassador recorded what would be his final diary entry. Clearly concerned for his safety, he bemoaned the "never ending security threats."[180] That evening he met with Turkish Consul General Ali Sait Akin. The purpose of the meeting, Fox News later reported, was "to negotiate a weapons transfer, an effort to get SA-7 missiles out of the hands of Libya-based extremists."[181]

At approximately half past eight, the ambassador escorted the Turkish diplomat to the compound gate. An hour later, at 9:35 p.m. local time, the assault began.

10

AMERICANS UNDER ASSAULT

A round nightfall, as 150 bearded gunmen in pickup trucks mounted with machine guns and bearing the insignia of Ansar al-Sharia began sealing off the streets leading to the U.S. mission facility in Benghazi, the militia and newly deputized police units in the area melted away.[182] Storming the Temporary Mission Facility (TMF) moments later, shouting "Alahu Akbar," the assailants would have been surprised—assuming they had not already been tipped off by informants inside—to find "a weak and very extended perimeter, an incomplete interior fence, no mantraps and unhardened entry gates and doors," as the Accountability Review Board (ARB) report later described the mission's physical security posture. Inside, they found a facility "severely under-resourced with regard to weapons, ammunition, non-lethal deterrents and fire safety equipment, including escape masks."[183]

Although in the fog of war and the welter of competing claims, much about precisely what occurred that night, and why, remains in dispute—or has been deliberately obscured—millions are familiar with the general parameters of the tragedy. How Ambassador

Stevens and information officer Sean Smith were led by Diplomatic Security Service (DSS) Special Agent Scott Strickland to the TMF's "safe haven" behind an impenetrable metal door but died by smoke inhalation after their Islamist murderers set the building afire. How the commandoes, stationed a mile away in the annex, were given conflicting orders and arrived too late. How by midnight the annex itself came under heavy attack, resulting in the deaths by mortar fire of defenders Glen Doherty and Tyrone Woods, who had stationed themselves on the building's roof.

Typically, the Obama administration sought to evade responsibility for the Benghazi debacle. Starting with its ludicrous tale of the attack as a frenzied mob reaction to an obscure anti-Islamic video by a California-based Christian Egyptian filmmaker, the administration has from the very outset been the opposite of forthcoming with both congressional investigators and the rare journalists who wrestle to pry loose the real facts. Yet for all the obfuscations and outright falsehoods, a simple fact was increasingly inescapable—the same one that has run through this administration's Middle East policies from the start: Members of the Obama administration refuse to recognize the bottomless evil of the Islamist enemy. Its malevolence. Its capacity for cruelty. Its willingness to lie in the service of its ends. Above all, that its aims are never strictly local or even national, but global.

Indeed, in that sense what happened in Benghazi on September 11, 2012, was exceptional only in the shock, grief, and anger it rightly aroused in America, for it was a result of the very policy thinking that had given rise to supporting the "rebels" in the first place and that, even afterward would hasten their control of the country.

That night, the administration's willful blindness about the nature of the jihadist threat was perhaps most tellingly exemplified by the trust it placed in the Islamic units charged with defending the ambassador's compound. A State Department official had blandly described the February 17th Martyrs Brigade as "a friendly militia . . . deputized by the Libyan government to serve as our security."[184]

Although in fact the group had shown itself relatively reliable in handling smaller-scale security, its having been given control of key checkpoints leading to the TMF and other Western facilities was a disaster waiting to happen.

On the night of the attack, February 17 failed to perform any of its assigned functions. The ARB report found "little evidence that February 17 contributed meaningfully to the defense of the Special Mission compound," and "little evidence that the armed February 17 guards alerted Americans at the [TMF] to the attack or summoned a February 17 militia presence to assist expeditiously once the attack was in progress."[185] Although a few dozen February 17 militiamen did join the CIA team when it belatedly reached the compound, they refused a request to provide covering fire, saying that they preferred to negotiate with jihadists inside.[186] In fact, even as the attack was in progress, the February 17th Martyrs Brigade Facebook page proclaimed that its fighters stood down and were not involved in attacking the "youth" (*shebab*).[187] The ARB report also found little evidence that February 17 "contributed meaningfully to . . . the evacuation to the airport" that took place the morning of September 12.[188]

Indeed, far from impeding the attack, the likelihood is high that February 17 commanders gave their blessing to Ansar al-Sharia's actions, perhaps believing the strike would be a limited one that would strengthen their leverage over Stevens in their ongoing protest over working conditions.[189] A copy of Stevens's itinerary discovered in the wreckage by a *Washington Post* reporter shows that he had had a scheduled meeting with a February 17 commander at 11:00 a.m. on the morning of September 11, but it had apparently been canceled. The words "another day" were handwritten next to the entry.[190]

The behavior of February 17 militiamen manning checkpoints near the TMF likewise suggests some degree of complicity in the attack. As DCM Gregory Hicks testified, "certainly, elements of that militia were complicit in the attacks," for the invaders "had to make a long approach march through multiple checkpoints that were manned by February 17 militia."[191] Previous knowledge of property details would have allowed the attackers to zero in on the diesel fuel canisters that they used to set the fire that killed Stevens.

The attackers themselves appeared to accept February 17 fighters as "friendlies." One of the Libyan guards later recounted that he told the attackers, "I am [a member] of the February 17 Brigade. Don't attack me . . . don't shoot," and was left in peace.[192]

The two quasi-official security forces operating under the control of the interior ministry and the defense ministry, the Supreme Security Committee (SSC) and the Libya Shield, had also been given roles in providing security for the TMF. Both had strong Islamist leanings, with members' having been implicated in numerous attacks of extremist violence, kidnappings, and assassinations.

The ARB report flatly describes the SSC as a "coalition of militia elements loosely cobbled into a single force to provide interim security—but in reality run by a diverse group of local Islamist militias, each of whose strength ebbed and flowed depending on the ever-shifting alliances and loyalties of various members."[193]

Two incidents earlier in the day of the attack further suggest complicity by SSC operatives. First, personnel in the TMF observed a uniformed SSC officer taking photos of the compound from the second story of an adjacent property. When approached, the man sped away in an SSC marked police car.[194] The incident was reported to the local February 17th Martyrs Brigade station—but there was no response. Sean Smith, the IT specialist who would die with Stevens, actually posted online about the episode prior to the attack: "[A]ssuming we don't die tonight. We saw one of our 'police' that guard the compound taking pictures."[195]

Then, just minutes before the attack, the SSC police car parked outside the compound abruptly departed. An SSC official later claimed that he ordered the removal of the car "to prevent civilian casualties."

As for Libya Shield, the group's powerful and notoriously violent commander Wissam bin Hamid (also known as bin Ahmed) arrived at the scene some thirty minutes after the start of the attack but, claiming "the situation wasn't suitable for me to go inside the compound,"[196] made no evident effort to stop it. In fact, no SSC or Libya Shield units meaningfully engaged the attackers at all.

It is also notable that according to a U.S. embassy diplomatic cable, two days earlier, on September 9, Libya Shield 1 commander Hamid and Libya Shield 2 commander Muhammad al-Gharabi had met with American security officials and urged them to support for prime minister the Muslim Brotherhood–linked Minister of Electricity Awad al-Barasi—who would appoint February 17 commander Fawzi Bukatef as minister of defense. The commanders threatened that they would be unable to guarantee security in Benghazi if the secularist Jibril won the post.[197]

Moreover, the hiring of five privately contracted guards, who performed poorly on the night of the attack, remains riddled with mystery. No guards "were present outside the compound immediately before the attack ensued, although perimeter security was one of their responsibilities, and there is conflicting information as to whether they sounded any alarms prior to fleeing the C1 gate area," the ARB reported, adding that "the speed with which attackers entered [the TMF] raised the possibility that . . . guards left the C1 pedestrian gate open after initially seeing the attackers and fleeing the vicinity. They had left the gate unlatched before."[198]

In fact, it is highly probable the guards provided pre-attack intelligence on the compound to the attackers. RSO Eric Nordstrom testified that security guards had not been vetted and that he had conveyed this concern to Washington. "Certainly we had also raised the issue of doing some sort of counter-intelligence vetting of the people that worked for us. Ultimately that was turned down too."[199]

"We weren't told they wanted more security," insisted Joe Biden in the vice presidential debate, exactly a month to the day after the attacks. "We did not know they wanted more security."[200] Extraordinary as this claim was, it was of course entirely consistent with the modus operandi of an administration in which blame-shifting has long been both a strategy and a reflex and that has, with the connivance of a friendly media, too often managed to dodge full responsibility for even its most blatant failures.

Still, even by the administration's own standards, the buck passing surrounding the attack at Benghazi has been staggeringly brazen. In testimony before the House Foreign Affairs Committee, the official charged with direct responsibility for the diplomatic mission in Benghazi, former secretary of state Clinton, acknowledged only that there were "inadequacies and problems in the responsiveness of our team here in Washington to the security requests that were made by our team in Libya," but she specifically disavowed any personal responsibility. "I was not aware of that going on, it was not brought to my attention, but obviously it's something we're fixing."[201] Unsurprisingly, this was contradicted by an April 2013 interim report by five House committees investigating the Benghazi tragedy, which concluded that "reductions of security levels prior to the attacks in Benghazi were approved at the highest levels of the State Department, up to and including Secretary Clinton."

Nonetheless, in the official report on Benghazi prepared for the State Department by the ARB, only four mid-level officials were reprimanded: Deputy Assistant Secretary for Diplomatic Security Charlene Lamb, Assistant Secretary of State for Diplomatic Security Eric Boswell, Principal Deputy Assistant Secretary of Diplomatic Security Scott Bultrowicz (their superior), and Deputy Assistant Secretary for Maghreb Affairs Raymond Maxwell (whose immediate superior, then Principal Deputy Assistant Secretary for Near Eastern Affairs Elizabeth Dibble, was not only not faulted, but later received a prestigious assignment as deputy chief of mission at the U.S.

embassy in London).[202] All four were placed on administrative leave, then reinstated in August 2013 by Secretary of State John Kerry, citing "no breach of duty."[203]

Maxwell, long an Obama loyalist, later directly contradicted the report, telling congressional investigators that he had played no role in the approval or rejection of security requests. Even more significantly, in September 2014, he made the bombshell claim that while the official report was being prepared, he had personally witnessed Clinton aides going through boxes of State Department files on Benghazi after hours, removing any that cast the Secretary or her department "in a bad light." "I was not invited to that after-hours endeavor," he said, "but I heard about it and decided to check it out on a Sunday afternoon." Damningly, he said that among those overseeing the "scrubbing" operation were two of those closest to Clinton, Cheryl Mills and Jake Sullivan.

Surely the most extraordinary claim in the ARB report was that Ambassador Stevens himself "did not see a direct threat of an attack of this nature and scale on the U.S. Mission" and that considering "his status as the leading U.S. government advocate on Libya policy, and his expertise on Benghazi," his superiors gave "unusual deference to his judgments."[204]

In the annals of blaming the victim, this case falls into the category of "beyond mind-boggling." Although, as Stevens's father observed in a postmortem op-ed, the ambassador certainly accepted that "there was a risk to being accessible,"[205] this in no way means that he judged the security in place in Benghazi to have been remotely acceptable. "Chris Stevens was not responsible for the reduction in security personnel. His requests for additional security were denied or ignored," wrote then DCM Hicks in a *Wall Street Journal* op-ed shortly after the release of the Senate Select Committee on Intelligence (SSCI) report. "The blame lies entirely with Washington."

Still, it is hardly surprising that the Obama administration has continued to dodge and lie and spin. The reality is simply too damning.

As for Hillary Clinton, she has perhaps a greater interest than anyone else in obscuring the truth. Republicans are seeking to hold her to account, with GOP presidential aspirant Rand Paul especially straightforward in his attacks: "Hillary's judgment has to be questioned," he says. "Her eagerness for war in Libya should preclude her from being considered the next commander in chief." Indeed, even within her own party, Ms. Clinton's role in the Libyan debacle continues to provoke harsh criticism, with former Senator Jim Webb, a possible (if unlikely) rival from the left, leading the way in condemning "our ever-changing entanglements of the Middle East, beginning with the Pandora's box that was opened with the invasion of Iraq and continuing through the illogical and still-fermenting nightmare of the Arab Spring, particularly our inadvisable actions in Libya."

In such circumstances, Hillary will surely continue doing what she does best—feverishly bobbing and weaving, seeking to avoid the issue entirely with the help of a compliant media.

If only she and the president had put nearly as much effort into pursuing a sensible Libyan policy in the first place.

11

THE AFTERMATH

Solving the murder of Ambassador Stevens and the three other Americans in Benghazi should not have been difficult. It was clear that Ansar al-Sharia, whose emblazoned trucks were seen by numerous witnesses, had played a lead role in the attack, and surveillance cameras at the Temporary Mission Facility (TMF) photographed sixty different attackers,[206] many clearly enough to identify them individually. Libya's then-president Mohammed Magarief readily acknowledged that "Al Qaida elements" bore responsibility[207] for the "pre-calculated, pre-planned attack that was carried out specifically to attack the U.S. Consulate."[208] Within a week, Libyan officials claimed to have identified fifty attackers by name and to have arrested four.[209]

A functioning government would have had the case cracked in no time. But it was equally clear that Libya did not have such a government—and, moreover, that the circle of those aiding and abetting the assault reached deep into the country's power structure. Days after the attack, two American intelligence officials told *Daily Beast* reporter Eli Lake that the United States had a September 11, 2012, intercept of a pro–Al Qaeda Libyan politician ordering a February 17 officer to have his men stand down for an imminent attack.[210]

The U.S. mission site itself was left unsecured for several days after the attack, allowing looters and others to pick through the rubble at their leisure (a CNN reporter found Stevens's diary), and fully three weeks passed[211] before the FBI was at the crime scene. After finally securing access to the site, the agents spent only twelve hours there before departing.[212]

Nevertheless, within six months, the agency had reportedly distinguished forty-five individuals from TMF and annex security footage as participants in the assault, of whom roughly twenty-five had been positively identified.[213] In May 2013, the FBI released photos of unidentified suspects and persons of interest, appealing to the Libyan public at large for assistance.[214] "We need your help to solve this crime," said a web page in English, with Arabic translation,[215] pointing to a follow-up tip page.[216]

But in an atmosphere where local militias held sway, media outlets did little to enlist the public's support for the campaign. Asked whether they had seen the photos, not one of the locals interviewed in an August 2013 CNN special acknowledged having seen them.[217] The FBI declined to list Benghazi suspects on its Rewards for Justice website, which offered substantial sums for tips leading to wanted terrorists. "Whether we pay a couple million dollars isn't the point—the point is we believe it's a priority . . . and whether they are on a website or not doesn't change that," State Department spokeswoman Marie Harf told reporters.[218]

Nor was the impotent Libyan government much more helpful. As the Senate Select Committee on Intelligence (SSCI) report later concluded, the government by now lacked "the political incentive or will within its own country to seek out, arrest, and prosecute individuals believed to be associated with the attacks."[219] Indeed, in June 2013, the authorities released, for lack of evidence, the only suspect then in their custody,[220] Faraj al-Chalabi, whose name had appeared alongside bin Laden's on the 1998 Interpol warrant filed by the Gaddafi regime.[221]

The reticence of both citizens and government authorities was understandable. Citing then–FBI director Robert Mueller, the SSCI report notes that "as many as 15 individuals supporting the investigation or otherwise helpful to the United States have been killed in Benghazi since the attacks, underscoring the lawless and chaotic circumstances in eastern Libya,"[222] adding that it is "unclear whether their killings were related to the Benghazi investigation."[223]

In August 2013, the U.S. Justice Department filed charges against an unspecified number of suspects in a sealed indictment.[224] Although it was widely leaked that Ansar al-Sharia leader Ahmed Abu Khattala was among those charged,[225] the identities of the others remained a closely guarded secret. Though Abu Khattala was singled out as the prime suspect, he made no effort to avoid the spotlight. In interviews with CNN and the *New York Times*, he offered praise for Al Qaeda while denying involvement in the attack.[226] In August, he claimed that he had not even been questioned by Libyan, let alone U.S., authorities.[227]

It was not until mid-June 2014, fully twenty-one months after the Benghazi attacks, that American Delta Force special operations commandos finally seized Abu Khattala and spirited him back to the United States to face criminal charges. Meanwhile, numerous other suspects remain at large, and there is little indication that most have anything to fear.[228]

Need anything more be said about the power of the jihadist militias in today's Libya—or about the impotence of the American government that so recently enabled their victory?

12

HOW?

"How could this happen in a country we helped liberate, in a city we helped save from destruction?"

—Secretary of State Hillary Clinton

This plaintive question, which came in the aftermath of the attack in Benghazi, is all the more startling for being posed by the one individual who should have been best positioned to anticipate what might happen that terrible night: Secretary of State Hillary Clinton. That she and her colleagues so utterly failed to grasp the risk at hand speaks directly to the ultimate, and deadliest, failure of understanding that besets the administration even now: the continuing refusal to grasp the very nature of the Islamist threat. For in choosing, at key moments, to lend American support to jihadists rather than to their foes (including even despicable ones, such as Muammar Gaddafi), the results were preordained. We were not (as the credulous, short-sighted administration policymakers in Washington insisted) advancing democratic values and ensuring the lasting peace: We were doing precisely the opposite.

That is apparent not just in the hell that is today's Libya, but also throughout other parts of the region and the world, where the same feckless policy choices been made since. We see it in Nigeria, where Boko Haram wantonly spreads terror, killing thousands and sending thousands more into slavery. We see it in Gaza, where Hamas heedlessly sacrifices civilians to vilify the single democratic state in the region and speed its eradication. And, of course, we see it in Iraq and Syria, where ISIS continues to explore new depths of savage barbarity. All these have vividly demonstrated time and again that in the worldwide caliphate envisaged by the jihadists, there are indeed no borders.

It is not as if America's enemies have been subtle over the past several decades about their methods or their intentions. As writer and Middle East expert Amir Taheri bluntly put it in September, 2014: "The capture of the US Embassy in Teheran, the attack on the USS Cole, the mass murder of US Marines in their sleeping quarters in Beirut, the destruction of US embassies in Kenya and Tanzania, the 9/11 attacks, the murder of countless GIs by IEDs in Afghanistan or Iraq, the beheading of Daniel Pearl in Pakistan, Nick Berg in Iraq and Paul Johnson in Saudi Arabia . . . [are] all fruits of a culture that has declared total war on America." In having so long failed to appreciate this fundamental fact, the Obama administration has demonstrated a naïveté that can be fairly said to border on criminal delusion.

Within Libya itself, the chaos and absence of minimal government authority today is impossible for even the Obama administration to deny. "We will not accept the project of democracy, secular parties, nor the parties that falsely claim the Islamic cause," the jihadist militias boldly declared in a joint statement, confident that they had nothing to fear from their former allies in the West.

In late May 2014, little more than three years after NATO began aiding the country's Islamist rebels, the State Department responded to the deteriorating situation by issuing a call to all U.S. citizens in the country to depart immediately, warning that "[the] Libyan government has not been able to adequately build its military and police forces and improve security following the 2011 revolution." Staffing at the U.S. embassy was cut to a bare minimum.

Three months later, in August, with a coalition of Islamist militias, including Ansar al-Sharia, bearing down on the capital, even that skeleton crew was removed from the country—and soon afterward, Americans watching at home were briefly distracted from images of the horrors being wrought by rampaging ISIS savages in Iraq to those of their Libyan Islamist militant brethren happily cavorting in the pool of the abandoned American embassy. The yawning vacuum America left behind in Libya had been definitively filled.

"A monstrous little dictator was removed," *Wall Street Journal* columnist Peggy Noonan mournfully observed, "which left an opening for people who were more monstrous still, who murdered our ambassador, burned our consulate in Benghazi, and now have run us out of Tripoli. What did the president absorb from this that now affects his thinking?"

Indeed, have Mr. Obama and Mrs. Clinton absorbed any lessons at all from the Libyan debacle? Even now there is little reason to suggest that they have. As late as December 2014, addressing a friendly audience, the former secretary of state talked of "[u]sing every possible tool and partner to advance peace and security. Leaving no one on the sidelines. Showing respect even for one's enemies. Trying to understand, in so far as psychologically possible, empathize with their perspective and point of view. Helping to define the problems, determine the solutions. That is what we believe in the 21st century will change—change the prospects for peace."[229]

Even a longtime supporter such as my respected colleague and former top Democrat on the House Intelligence Committee, Jane Harman of California, said that she was puzzled by Clinton's statement. "I take issue with the word 'enemies,'" Harman told Fox's Chris Wallace. "I think we have to respect people with different points of view in order to win the argument with them. I don't exactly know what she was saying." She continued, "I don't think we have to respect members of terror groups ever. I think we have to have harsh policies against them."[230]

But, addressing the 2014 U.S. Islamic World Forum on September 15, with the region aflame and the entire world on edge, Assistant Secretary of State for Near Eastern Affairs Anne Patterson doubled down. There are those, she intoned, echoing the president's own perverse refusal to call evil by its rightful name, who "conflate Islamists with terrorists and desire to eliminate the Islamists from the political scene," adding that "our difficult fight against violent extremists is made more complicated by this viewpoint."

And still they're wondering why nothing has gone right.

13

LESSONS LEARNED

A popularly quoted description of insanity is repeating the same thing over and over again and expecting a different result. The basis for sound governmental policy is precisely the opposite: studying previous actions for what worked and what didn't, then drawing the appropriate conclusions. With that in mind, and looking toward the future, it is vital to focus now on the lessons that we as a nation have learned, or should have learned, from our actions over the past thirty years in the Middle East.

While I was working with Whip and then Speaker Newt Gingrich as part of his planning team, Gingrich was obsessed with the military concept of lessons learned—so much so that I actually spent a couple of days at the Army's Training and Doctrine Center (TRADOC) to learn more about the process. "Lessons learned" is a concept employed by business management and the military to review past activities and apply the insights gained to future situations and decisions. Knowledge management consultant Nick Milton defines lessons learned as a change in personal or operational behavior as a result of experience. He suggests a series of steps that include reflecting on events; identifying learning points; analyzing differences between plans and outcomes, then generalizing them to apply to future activity; and recommending specific action to improve performance.[231]

The U.S. military created its own department on the subject, the Center for Army Lessons Learned at the U.S. Army Combined Arms Center, which takes the concept a few steps further. It offers minutely detailed schematics, diagrams, and procedures for exploiting experiences through "identifying, collecting, analyzing, disseminating, and archiving issues and best practices; and by maintaining situational awareness in order to share knowledge throughout the Army as well as our unified action partners utilizing tools like networks, workshops, and interviews."[232]

Stephen M. Walt, a professor of international relations at Harvard University, argues that President Obama and his administration forgot lessons previously learned on the limits of American power and so never anticipated the mess they'd create by removing Muammar Gaddafi.[233] If, indeed, they are at last open to the lessons learned concept, then the resulting chaos and failed Libyan state might help them avoid repeating the same mistakes in the future. But, of course, whether this is in fact the case remains very much an open question.

On assuming office in January 2009, Barack Obama claimed that he would be the president who would end the wars in the Middle East and, moreover, stop doing "stupid stuff." Those claims have now been laid bare as having been entirely baseless. For one thing, the war Obama inherited in Iraq, though it had certainly taken a heavy toll on the national psyche, had by then largely blunted the jihadist threat in the country: All that remained was maintaining a residual force sufficient to guarantee those hard-won gains. Instead, when SEAL Team Six took down Osama Bin Laden in May 2011, the president, in full campaign mode, declared victory and recklessly withdrew all American troops from Iraq. His feckless policies predictably led to the rise of ISIS, leaving us in greater peril than ever; even he now concedes that the fight against resurgent and ever more murderous jihadism could take years.

Yet even today, this president steadfastly refuses to call the enemy by its rightful name—or to acknowledge that the fight against this latest strain of radical Islam is only an extension of the one that began more than thirty-five years ago, with the November 1979 takeover of the American Embassy in Iran and the 400-plus-day hostage crisis that ensued. Although over the years the Islamic threat to America and its interests has ebbed and flowed, it has never—not for a moment—abated.

Along the way, of course, have been dramatic successes, notably the elimination of much of core Al Qaeda and the killing of bin Laden himself. But it is the current administration's failure to capitalize and build on those successes that has resulted in failures almost as spectacular in the Middle East, in Africa, and, yes, even at home. Like it or not, we must deal with these now, learning the lessons of the recent past—for the consequences of not doing so are beyond unthinkable.

LESSON 1:
THE PROBLEM IS RADICAL ISLAM!

This was never about Gitmo, waterboarding, or even Israel. Radical jihadists despise us, our culture, our political system, and our way of life. They believe in jihad, the caliphate, and the imposition of *sharia* law—all incompatible with our way of life. But as more recent events have clearly demonstrated by brutal beheadings, rape, and countless other acts of brutality, radical jihadists hate everyone who does not subscribe to their worldview. They target their violence especially at Christians and other religious minorities in the Middle East, and their vicious actions also extend to those Muslims who do not share the radical jihadists' worldview.

Crucially, this is a lesson that conservatives, too, have had a great deal of trouble learning—it was, after all, George W. Bush who repeatedly proclaimed Islam a "religion of peace." And although his intentions were clear and even admirable—to avoid being seen as attacking the overwhelming majority of Muslims, who go about their lives peaceably, and to emphasize and celebrate the many human qualities that we all have in common—such a formulation also left too many things unsaid.

What needed to be said was that parts of Islam *were* at war with the West and others who do not share their ideology. That the threat from "radical" Islam was real. That even if the West confronted the threat militarily, defeating this enemy would require leaders in the Muslim community who were willing to confront the cancer within Islam.

I have met many Middle Eastern Muslims who love America, who respect our culture and our society. They do not seek to overthrow it or destroy it. In many cases, they hope to integrate parts of it into their own societies, though they recognize that doing so will be a long process and one that must be worked from within rather than imposed by outsiders.

They are even open to tolerance of other religions, if perhaps not to the extent that we in the West desire. Indeed, in many parts of the Middle East there once *was* a certain religious tolerance: For centuries, Chaldeans, Copts, Jews, and other religious minorities survived in Muslim-majority countries. They were protected. But all that has changed: A different Islam, radical jihadism, has widely taken root in the Middle East. That Islam terrorizes religious minorities, "cleansing" vast geographic areas by murdering those who are not of the Islamic faith.

The West must deal with this harsh reality, as well as with the attitudes that this reality has engendered throughout the region—attitudes that were all too evident in a massive survey of more than 38,000 ordinary people in thirty-nine Muslim or largely Muslim countries. Although the degree of intolerance varied from country to country, the data, blandly recorded at length in the report, is nonetheless staggering to the Western mind: "[H]igh percentages in all the countries surveyed support making *sharia* the official law, including nearly universal support among Muslims in Afghanistan (99%). More than eight-in-ten Muslims in Pakistan (84%) and Bangladesh (82%) also hold this view . . . substantial proportions of Muslims support severe punishments such as cutting off the hands of thieves or stoning people who commit adultery . . . . at least half of Muslims who favor making *sharia* the law of the land also favor stoning unfaithful spouses . . . in 10 of 20 countries where there are adequate samples for analysis[,] at least half say they support penalties such as whippings or cutting off the hands of thieves and robbers . . . in six of the 20 countries where there are adequate samples for analysis, at least half of those who favor making Islamic law the official law also support executing apostates . . . . In the South Asian countries of Afghanistan and Pakistan, strong majorities of those who favor making Islamic law the official law of the land also approve of executing apostates (79% and 76%, respectively) . . . . Taking the life of those who abandon Islam is most widely supported in Egypt (86%) and Jordan (82%). Roughly two-thirds who want sharia to be the law of the land also back this penalty in the Palestinian territories (66%) . . . ." Tellingly, although—as noted—the survey included some of the most purportedly pro-Western countries in the region, including such American allies as Egypt and Jordan, arguably the most rigidly orthodox nations of all, Iran and Saudi Arabia, were not included.

Indeed, it was precisely the refusal of the Bush administration to take seriously or understand the realities of Muslim culture that led it to grossly underestimate the enormous obstacles that it faced in seeking to foster Western-style democracies in that part of the world. Although the policy ultimately succeeded militarily thanks to the skill of our military as well as thanks to Bush's own political tenacity, by the time those gains were jeopardized by Bush's successor, more than 5,000 American lives had been sacrificed. There is no question that it will always be recorded as a misadventure. We will never know how Iraq would have turned out had a residual force of American troops stayed behind.

LESSON 2:
PREPARE FOR THE LONG WAR,
BECAUSE CHANGE IS HARD

Radical jihadists hate us. Their hatred is intractable, not subject to compromise or reason. Difficult as the thought might be to accept for those of us in the West, we must be psychologically prepared to continue to fight for as long as it takes. The ideology must be confronted and changed from within the Islamic community; it cannot be imposed from the outside.

President Obama stated early on in his presidential campaign that if only he were president, the radical extremists would behave differently—implying that it was not our country or its values that they hated, but simply President Bush. He, Barack Hussein Obama, would get them to like America again.

In fact, what America must learn, finally and without equivocation, is that the jihadists hate us for who we are and for how we live. It was not for nothing that back in 1979 Ayatollah Khomeini declared America the Great Satan—this even though he himself had come to power largely as a result of the hopelessly naïve policies of another American president, Jimmy Carter. Hatred of America and the West was Khomeini's stock in trade, and it remains that of his successors, as they have repeatedly demonstrated—not only by their rhetoric, but also by their support of terrorists in the region, including those who murdered 241 American servicemen and sixty-four others in the 1983 bombing of the Marine barracks in Beirut.

And yes, their hatred is as strong today under Barack Obama as it was under Ronald Reagan—which leads to our next lesson. It will take a strong, focused effort by Islamic religious leaders to confront and defeat the ideology of radical jihadists. Until that happens, the threat will continue and grow.

This is more than about winning militarily. An ideology must be defeated. Defeating an ideology and its proponents takes decades.

LESSON 3:
THERE ARE LESSER EVILS

Geopolitical affairs are rarely black or white. They are usually shades of gray, sometimes ones that are very hard to tell apart.

During my tenure on the Intelligence Committee, I traveled to more than eighty countries, sometimes meeting with leaders rightly reputed as being among the harshest and most oppressive in the world. Much as I may have despised their behavior and their governance, I realized that my primary responsibility was ensuring the safety and security of the United States and its people. And sometimes we needed such leaders to help us achieve our national security goals. Odious as they were, they were the lesser of two evils. They were the devil we knew. If they disappeared from the scene, there was no telling what would follow—but sometimes we could hazard a pretty good guess.

It was on that basis, for instance, that we forged fragile relations with Islam Karimov in Uzbekistan—because we needed supply lines into Afghanistan from the north to fight an effective war there. We forged strong relationships with Hosni Mubarak in Egypt to maintain stability and peace along Israel's southern border—a relationship and friendship that proved invaluable during the Iraqi and Afghan wars. The long relationship with Egypt was an enduring relationship that benefited Egypt, the United States, Israel, and the entire rest of the region. And yes, we formed a relationship with Muammar Gaddafi in

Libya so that we could have a strong ally in northern Africa, prevent the spread of the radical threat into the Sahel and Maghreb, and provide a security buffer to the soft underbelly of Europe. These three examples show how the United States engaged with a wide range of countries and leaders to protect our national security interests and bring stability to the Middle East.

Although none of these relationships was perfect, there is no question that each helped keep America and the West safer. The relationships also enabled the United Staes to more effectively use its influence to bring about reforms in the political and human rights arenas.

LESSON 4:
UNDERSTAND THE ENVIRONMENT

Shortly before the 2007 surge in Iraq, when the Sunni tribes were helping Al Qaeda and anti-U.S. forces, a friend invited me to Jordan to meet with Sunni leaders. For three days I talked with the Iraqi Sunni chieftains, and over and over I heard the same thing: "We have our system, and you have yours. We have our values, and you have yours. We have a system of local government that has worked for thousands of years: It is called the tribal system. Do not try to impose your system on ours. We don't want it, and we don't need it. I'm the leader of the tribe, and if you think that you can impose democratic electoral reforms at the local level, we will continue to fight you and your allies."

Shortly thereafter, General David Petraeus took heed, formulating a campaign explicitly on such a basis to make it clear to the local Sunnis that America was suspending efforts at democratization at the local level and would respect existing structures and practices. The Sunni tribes participated in the surge, and the rest is history.

Clearly, the United States and other Western nations must recognize that the same holds true almost everywhere we've been fighting radical Islam. Local customs and traditional methods of governance cannot be bent to our will. Although from our perspective they may seem far from perfect—in some cases, even primitive and cruel—what matters is that they are embraced by the local population.

It is vital to always seek to understand the local perspective. Indeed, the locals understand, even if we too often forget, that many of the countries in the region are artificial constructs, put together after World War I for no other reason than to serve European convenience; what is permanent are the tribes, sects, and ethnicities of the peoples who inhabit the region.

If such countries are ever to change fundamentally, we must understand that their change will be a long and exceedingly slow process. Furthermore, it will be locally driven, not imposed by outsiders.

LESSON 5:
YOU BREAK IT, YOU OWN IT (AND THE COST WILL BE HIGH)

Post-9/11, the United States broke Afghanistan and Iraq. At the time, the reasons for those wars seemed entirely understandable. Three thousand Americans were dead, and the Taliban had blood on its hands—and who could doubt that they or the terrorists they sponsored would spill more? They had to be rooted out at the source—Afghanistan.

In hindsight, whether Saddam Hussein also needed to be stopped in light of his proven capacity for creating trouble in the region and otherwise doing great evil was a far more difficult question. Did it warrant a vast American investment in blood and treasure? Was it even a legitimate part of the war on terror?

Let's get directly to the issue that aroused such rancorous discord at the time: Did Saddam, in fact, possess weapons of mass destruction? Even now, after all the years of charges and countercharges, the answer is unclear. Certainly no significant evidence was unearthed that the Iraqi dictator was on his way to achieving nuclear capability. On the other hand, as I learned back in 2005, as chairman of the House Permanent Select Committee on Intelligence, the military had unearthed hundreds of chemical weapons shells in Iraq, a discovery that the Bush administration, foolishly preferring (as Karl Rove put it) to "let sleeping dogs lie," withheld from the public. In short, there was a cover-up—driven by politics, but perpetrated also by the military—that certainly dramatically affected the public debate on Iraq.

What we do know all these years later is that in the wake of America's departure, today's Iraq *is* a disaster of incalculable proportions, with ISIS in control of a significant swath of the country and committing horrific atrocities on a scale that no one could have imagined. We owned Iraq for a time, but we left before the job of rebuilding was done—assuming that it could have ever been completed.

And the Afghanistan we are now leaving is little different from the Afghanistan we inherited. It is an Afghanistan where, with more than 50 percent of the national economy fueled by the illegal drug trade, a civil society living by the rule of law—in other words, the Afghanistan we sought to create—remains a fantasy. Only time will tell how Afghanistan will turn out. What we broke in those conflicts, with the most idealistic of expectations but ultimately at such an excruciatingly high cost to both ourselves and the Afghan population, we owned only briefly.

Then there's Libya. Failing to grasp the fundamental lesson of those earlier experiences—that once broken, a nation is very difficult to put back together—President Obama broke Libya. Worse, in this case, some would say that the United States actually supported the wrong side, overthrowing an ally in the war against radical Islam in favor of the jihadists. After all, Gaddafi was killed only six months after Osama Bin Laden. And afterward we made an even more serious mistake—by showing zero interest in owning what we'd broken. Little wonder that Libya has become the disaster it is, not only further destabilizing the region, but exposing the soft under-belly of Europe—and much of Africa—to radical jihadists.

When you break it, not only do you own it, but you also have a responsibility to fix it or suffer the consequences—whatever they may be.

LESSON 6:
A PRESIDENT MUST LEAD

The U.S. Constitution not only allows, but in fact requires, Congress to have a say in the conduct of war and foreign policy, and many articulate voices have spoken about the war on terror in both the Senate and the House. The leaders of certain committees, especially Foreign Affairs, Armed Services, and Intelligence, help set the parameters of foreign and national security policy.

But in matters of war and peace, there is one voice that matters vastly more than all 535 members of Congress combined. For the president has by far the biggest megaphone with which to reach and influence the public, and as commander-in-chief, the president takes the lead in how war is conducted. It is the president to whom the international community looks for leadership, and the American people expect to find it in him. The president sets the tone and tenor for foreign policy, and the president conducts the orchestra.

Moreover, as far back as Vietnam, the presidency has expanded its powers under the War Powers Act. The president is expected to use those powers judiciously. But the president must lead—defining who our enemies are and how, and whether, to confront them.

We have all seen far too clearly the results when the president, out of fecklessness or inexperience or misplaced ideology, abdicates presidential responsibility. Presidents are expected to lead and need to lead if American foreign policy is to be effective.

LESSON 7:
HUMBLE PIE, ANYONE?

America's political leaders need to realize that foreign policy is hard. It is very, very difficult. It is time to learn that we have been wrong about foreign policy as often as we have been right. Today, we must look back at the last twenty years and recognize that the world is not what was envisioned after the collapse of the former Soviet Union. Many expected a time of peace and prosperity—a much calmer and safer world with fewer trouble spots. But the world has not turned out that way.

Few, if any, would have predicted or anticipated that in 2015, Libya, Iraq, Syria, and Yemen would all be on the verge of being failed states, their central governments having lost control of major territory within their borders to insurgent groups. Few would have predicted the aggressive posture now demonstrated by Russia. And did anyone really anticipate that the radical jihadist movement would expand to include groups in Nigeria and other parts of Africa?

American leaders also need to become better listeners. Many of our friends and allies around the world have attempted to advise and help us. Too often their comments either were never really heard or were outright disregarded. America's foreign policy would be enhanced if active listening were a part of our foreign policy DNA.

Although much of American political dialogue has focused on who did what wrong, it should be apparent to all that many political leaders have erred in their policy recommendations and actions. There is enough blame to go around. Now is the time for a genuine, serious dialogue about how to move forward collectively. Now is the time for everyone to eat a little humble pie, acknowledging that we have all been wrong at some point through this process.

LESSON 8:
FOREIGN POLICY MATTERS—A LOT

Typically, American elections are focused on domestic issues. This is to be expected: Foreign policy and national security issues are nearly always far down the list of poll-tested priorities. As James Carville straightforwardly put it in the reminder on the campaign bulletin board that helped get Bill Clinton elected, "It's the economy, stupid."

But foreign policy does matter. Always. And it matters immensely even in times of relative calm. Trade policies and tariffs have dramatic effects on the competitiveness of American industry—whether we will be domestic job creators or the destination of billions of dollars in imports. Stability or political unrest abroad likewise affects our economy in various and often unpredictable ways.

But in a time when the threat posed by radical Islam is ever more potent, foreign policy matters even more—far more. And voters must understand this reality. So must the candidates—especially the Republican presidential aspirants—who seek the voters' approval in 2016. This is a challenge to which one party, at least—the one that for half a century has led the way on national defense—must fully rise.

14

CONCLUSION:
THE BIG PICTURE

In the preceding chapter, I discussed lessons learned from the many policy mistakes made in Libya, focusing on issues that must henceforth be carefully evaluated by presidents, legislators, and foreign policy officials to avoid equally catastrophic blunders going forward. Yet perhaps the most vital lesson that must be learned, and one that must be continually relearned as we confront the threat of radical Islam, is that America needs a long-term strategy that is bipartisan.

For many years, such an understanding was so universal—indeed, so much a given—that its importance scarcely needed to be mentioned. The idea, as enunciated by Michigan Republican Senator Arthur Vandenberg in the tense aftermath of World War II, was that politics "stopped at the water's edge." In other words, when the country was under threat, it was imperative that both parties rally around the president's foreign policy to present a unified front to the world. A unified America couldn't effectively be challenged.

To be sure, there were times—notably, during the anguish and moral chaos of the Vietnam War era—when that consensus seemed to unravel. Indeed, I myself believe that "the water's edge" argument, though it certainly is an ideal worth striving for, can be oversold—because the actions of our political leaders, from the president on down, must always be held to scrutiny. Nonetheless, on balance, overwhelmingly, such a concept has served us remarkably well, especially with regard to genuine threats to America's self interest.

And so it long had in the Middle East. For decades, no matter which party was in power, American policy in that part of the world was unwavering: strong support for the state of Israel and opposition to Iran, Iraq, Libya, and states that fell into the Soviet orbit. At the same time, we forged long-term alliances with pro-American monarchies and dictatorships in the region; if they did not embrace all of our ideals of democracy and human rights, we hoped to slowly nudge them in the direction of reform.

In brief, there was both coherence and predictability to American Middle East policy. It wasn't always popular. We often stood almost alone backing Israel through decades of wars and political isolation. But the mold had been cast. Our policy was in place.

It was out of confident belief that that policy was firm and unchangeable that Libyan leader Muammar Gaddafi—a longtime practitioner of state-sponsored terror, a man who had ordered terrorist bombings that had destroyed two civilian airliners—made his fateful decision to change his spots and align his nation with the United States.

It was a gamble worth taking only because, seemingly, it wasn't much of a gamble at all. Indeed, America's invasion of Iraq in 2003 proved to Gaddafi that aligning with the United States not only would yield long-term security and economic benefits, but was crucial to his own survival. Should he continue to operate as he had, he believed, Libya would be the next target of a Bush administration that in the wake of the 9/11 attacks was determined to crush state-sponsored terror throughout the region. But if he played ball, the threat of a

U.S. invasion would disappear and, post-Iraq, Libya would benefit when American Middle East policy returned to the norm.

Alas, it is now all too clear that American Middle East foreign policy will never return to the Cold War–era norm. Indeed, the radical Islamist extremism loosed by the Iranian Revolution of 1979 has only steadily grown and metastasized—through the civil war in Lebanon and the bombing of the Marine barracks in Beirut during the Reagan years, through the first World Trade Center and Khobar Towers bombings, through the attacks on American embassies in Tanzania and Kenya and on the USS *Cole* during the Clinton years, and culminating in the tragedy of 9/11.

Yet it was only on that terrible September day more than fourteen years ago that we at last came to grips with the idea that we were at war with radical Islam. That infamous day was a horrific blow to America in multiple ways: economically, militarily, politically. Moreover, it was a psychological shock, altering the way we saw the world and our place in it.

For a time after 9/11, there was in America a terrific unity of purpose. The "water's edge" adage never seemed truer nor more apt, the parties putting aside their differences to come together in robust support of the fight against radical Islam. Democrats and Republicans worked side by side in approving tough counterterrorism measures and providing all the military resources needed to crush Al Qaeda in Afghanistan. Although Nancy Pelosi now denies it, this included signing off on such controversial programs as enhanced interrogation of foreign terrorist suspects. Like their Republican counterparts, most congressional Democrats supported the 2003 war with Iraq in the seemingly well-founded belief that Saddam Hussein had WMD programs and so was a looming threat to America. Having failed to "connect the dots" on intelligence prior to 9/11, there was a bipartisan determination not to make that fatal mistake again.

Unfortunately, on Iraq, the "dots" were wrong. The intelligence that President Bush relied on to invade Iraq was deeply flawed; U.S.

troops occupying Iraq failed to find evidence of nuclear, chemical, or biological weapons production. (Although evidence of older stockpiles of chemical weapons was found, the full extent of these discoveries would not be made public until 2014.[234])

Some supporters of President Bush continue to argue that overthrowing Saddam was nonetheless a worthy effort. I don't buy it. In addition to all the war's horrific consequences, beginning with its tremendous costs in blood and treasure, the Iraq war utterly shattered the post-9/11 bipartisan approach to U.S. national security.

Quite simply, driven by the trauma of the 9/11 attacks, we failed to understand, or to take the time to consider, the implications of where our Iraqi involvement was likely to lead. Before going to war in Iraq, I visited with the heads of state and chief intelligence leaders of just about every country that bordered Iraq. Almost to a person, they said the same thing: "You're making a huge mistake. You don't know what you will be unleashing." These allies, all of whom had supported sanctions and no-fly zones over Iraq, as well as international coalition efforts to roll back Saddam's 1991 invasion of Kuwait, understood the forces that would be unleashed by this dramatic shift in U.S. foreign policy. We did not.

The Iraq war—and the intelligence failures that gave it impetus—had consequences devastating to U.S. foreign policy. No longer wishing to be seen as having supported the war, liberals took up the mantra "Bush lied, people died"—a malicious falsehood that even as it helped effectively destroy the Bush presidency also put an end to any hope of bipartisan unity on Middle Eastern policy. One aspect of the liberal campaign against the president that was especially damaging involved frequent leaks of intelligence to the news media. Meanwhile, the political environment on the floor of the House and in committee hearings was poisonous, by far the worst it had ever been during my time in Congress. Every move President Bush tried to make on the international front, no matter its merits, was reflexively attacked by the left.

The effects of this deeply irresponsible behavior on our national security can hardly be overstated. Many Democratic members of Congress strongly condemned counterterrorism intelligence programs put in place by President Bush after 9/11—never mind that they had previously been thoroughly briefed on those very programs and enthusiastically endorsed them. Even though a bipartisan commission—the Robb/Silberman Commission—reported in 2005 that there had been serious problems with prewar intelligence on Iraq's WMD, Democrats persisted in claiming that the president and his senior officials had "lied" about Saddam's WMD programs. As much as anything else, this reflected Democrats' continuing and unceasing ire over the controversial election of 2000, whose results many still refused to accept.

The political acrimony in the aftermath of the Iraq war masked a second, even more significant consequence of the war: a major divide between the political parties on the threat from radical Islam. It became evident in the mid-2000s that Democrats and the liberal media flatly rejected the notion that radical Islam posed a deep and enduring threat to America itself, regarding any claim to that effect by the Bush administration as dishonest and self-justifying. To the contrary, they regarded any evidence of radicalism by Islamists as a consequence of, or a reaction to, the Bush administration's unjustified invasion of Iraq and, in due course, to the Guantanamo Bay detention center.

As we know all too well, even today President Obama refuses to use the terms "radical Islam" or "Islamist terrorist." Having come into office believing that he could be the anti-Bush, reaching out to the Muslim world and quelling Muslim extremism by apologizing for past U.S. foreign policy, Mr. Obama is caught in a trap of his own making. The chaotic aftermath of the Arab Spring, the collapse of U.S. Libyan policy, the rise of the Islamic State—all of it has to do, to one degree or another, with an approach on the part of this president that was self-deluded fantasy, doomed to failure.

To maintain his fantasy, President Obama has repeatedly ignored evidence of a rapidly expanding radical Islamist threat. His blinkered worldview led him to misunderstand what was happening in Egypt with the election of Islamist President Mohamed Morsi; in Syria, when civil war led to the rise of radical Islamist terrorist groups and training camps; in Yemen, where the government has steadily lost ground to Al Qaeda insurgents; and of course in Libya, where a lawless power vacuum has allowed armed militias and radical Islamist groups to proliferate. Under Obama, friends have needlessly become enemies, and enemies not worthy of trust are foolishly regarded as friends. We've thrown out dictators only to embrace far worse. American foreign policy has been turned upside-down.

We are in trouble. Many argue that the threats to the West are greater today than they were fourteen years ago, and it would be hard to prove them wrong. In no small part, this results from America's departure from a consistent and long-term foreign policy.

It is long past time for us to regain our foreign policy bearings, returning to a foreign policy that looks to defend our interests abroad and protect us against real and growing threats at home. In practice, this means that in the Middle East the United States will sometimes need to be aligned with unsavory leaders. It might even mean that the United States and its European allies will need to hold their noses and accommodate themselves to the likes of some of the unsavory leaders the Middle East has seen over the last 40 years, because, onerous as they are, the far graver threat to ourselves and the world at large is posed by the Islamic State.

But such an approach, if it is to succeed, will require strong bipartisan support. President Obama must drop his tendency to blame the Bush administration for instability in the Middle East and instead fully acknowledge the threat from radical Islam. Republicans, for their part, must agree to support the hard decisions that President Obama must make to salvage U.S. foreign policy in the Middle East.

Once again, America needs a strong foreign policy that is predictable, pragmatic, and understandable. In 2003, America badly miscalculated in Iraq, and—in ill-advised reaction, driven by rank partisanship—we've been making terrible mistakes in the region ever since. Libya is the best case study in this ongoing calamity. In vivid detail, it shows how America's wholly erratic behavior, from administration to administration and from one party's philosophy to the other's, has left us ever more ineffective and, ultimately, vulnerable.

This is unacceptable. The world needs a strong America—an America that understands who it is, what it will do, and what its power can, and cannot, achieve. Not the vacillating, unpredictable America of the last fourteen years, but an America confident enough in itself to consistently lead.

ROGUES' GALLERY

- **Abdel Hakim Belhadj (*nom de guerre Abu Abdullah al-Sadiq/Assadaq*):** Emir of LIFG; founder of February 17th Martyrs Brigade. Military leader of NTC. Member of Libyan Al Watan Party. See photograph at http://www.telegraph.co.uk/news/worldnews/africaandindianocean/libya/8999176/Libyan-commander-Abdelhakim-Belhadj-withdraws-cooperation-from-Britain-torture-inquiry.html.

- **Ali Al Sallabi:** Leading Islamic cleric. Chief negotiator for LIFG. Spiritual head of February 17th Martyrs Brigade. See photograph at http://www.telegraph.co.uk/news/worldnews/africaandindianocean/libya/8879955/Libyan-cleric-announces-new-party-on-lines-of-moderate-Islamic-democracy.html.

- **Ismail al-Sallabi:** Founder of February 17th Martyrs Brigade. Key figure in organizing Libyan terror training camps. See photograph at http://online.wsj.com/news/articles/SB10001424052970204002304576627000922764650.

- **Sami al Saadi:** Spiritual head of LIFG. Termed "the sheikh of the Arabs" by Mullah Omar of the Taliban. Author of LIFG's anti-democracy manifesto, *The Choice Is Theirs*. See photograph at http://www.itv.com/news/story/2012-12-13/uk-2-2m-libya-rendition-payout/.

- **Abdel Hakim al Hasadi:** Dernah commander. Captured in Pakistan in 2002. Rendered by the United States to

Libya in 2004. Released by Gaddafi in 2008. Recruited jihadists from eastern Libya to fight in Iraq. See photograph at https://veritasdomain.wordpress.com/category/people/abdel-hakim-al-hasadi/.

- **Sufian bin Qumu:** Head of Ansar al-Sharia Dernah, which took credit for the September 2012 attack. LIFG military commander and reputed former driver for Osama bin Laden. Apprehended by the United States and imprisoned in Guantanamo Bay, where a leaked 2008 JTF–GTMO Detainee Assessment indicated that he was "likely to pose a threat to the U.S., its interests and allies." Rendered back to Libya in September 2007. See photograph at http://shoebat.com/wp-content/uploads/2014/01/Sufian_bin_Qumu_Beard-e1389450329985.jpg.

- **Mahdi al Harati:** Among the most important rebel commanders of the Libyan civil war. Top associate of Belhadj, for whom he acted as operational commander. After Gaddafi's fall, went to Syria to arrange for troops, training, and weapons. Recently elected mayor of Tripoli. See photograph at http://www.nathanielturner.com/libyaislamicreformtable.htm.

- **Abdel Basit Haroun al Shahabi:** Commander of February 17th Martyrs Brigade. Later formed the Abu Salim Martyrs Brigade (renamed Darnah Martyrs Brigade). Accompanied the first shipment of Libyan weapons to Syria in April 2012. See photographs at http://www.thetimes.co.uk/tto/news/world/middleeast/article3088776.ece.

- **Wissam bin Hamid:** Commander of Libya Shield in Benghazi, under the umbrella of the February 17th Martyrs Brigade. Charged to provide security for Americans in Benghazi, though he had fought the Americans in both

Iraq and Afghanistan before returning to Libya. Has stated: "The Islamic shariah is a red line, we will not cede one rule of it, and Islam is the only law-giver and not [merely] the foundation [of the law]." See photographs at http://counterjihadreport.com/tag/hamid/.

- **Fawzi Bukatef:** Commander, February 17th Martyrs Brigade. Educated in Ohio. Was affiliated with the Muslim Brotherhood and imprisoned at Abu Salim by Gaddafi for eighteen years. Recruited and trained jihadist fighters. Implicated in the murder of a pro-Gaddafi French security contractor. See photograph at http://gulagbound.com/34933/the-real-why-of-benghazi-part-2/.

- **Mokhtar Belmokhtar:** Known as "The Uncatchable." A one-eyed Islamist who cut his teeth fighting the Soviets in Afghanistan in the 1980s. Leader of Al Qaeda in the Islamic Maghreb. Split from AQIM in 2013 and launched the Signatories in Blood, masterminding a raid of an Algerian gas plant during which thirty-eight hostages were killed in retaliation for French-led military intervention in Mali. See photographs at https://en.wikipedia.org/wiki/Mokhtar_Belmokhtar.

- **Abu Yahya al Libi-Qaid:** Top Al Qaeda operative in Libya. Tasked with forming *katibas*, or fighting battalions, as well as with coordinating with senior terrorist leaders abroad. Killed in a drone strike. See photograph at http://www.telegraph.co.uk/news/worldnews/al-qaeda/9312050/Al-Qaeda-leader-Abu-Yahya-al-Libi-target-of-US-drone-strike.html.

GLOSSARY

Abd al-Hakim al-Libi (also known as Mohammad Ahmad al-Shariah): LIFG fighter who died during the invasion of Afghanistan in October 2001, killed by U.S. forces in the battle for Kabul.

Abd al-Wahhab Qaid: Compatriot of Khalid al-Sharif. Appointed commander of the border guards in southern Libya.

Abd al-Wahhab Qaid: The brother of Abu-Yahya al-Libi. Released by the Gaddafi regime as one of the last 110 LIFG members still imprisoned, who either had refused to repent or were for other reasons considered too dangerous to be released.

Abdel-Hakim Belhadj (also known as Abu Abdullah al-Sadeq): Leader of the conservative Islamist al-Watan Party. Former head of the Tripoli Military Council and emir of LIFG.

Abdel-Raouf Al-Karah: Founder of the Nawasi Brigade.

Abdul Hakim al-Hasadi: LIFG commander who was arrested in Pakistan, handed over to the United States, and extradited to Libya.

Abdul Qadeer Khan: Pakistani nuclear scientist, more famous as Dr. A.Q. Khan.

Abdullah Sabir: Abdul Basit Azuz's lieutenant and a former LIFG member.

Abdul-Munim Mukhtar al-Madhun (also known as Urwah): Veteran LIFG commander who returned to Libya after the outbreak of the revolt to lead the 160-man Omar al-Mukhtar Battalion in eastern Libya until 2011.

Abu Abdullah al-Libi (also known as Osama al Obeidi): Major Libyan recruiter and commander in Syria, whose résumé includes stints in Algeria, Iraq, and Libya.

Abu al-Laith al-Libi (also known as Ali Ammar Ashur al-Raqiai): One of Al Qaeda's leading military chiefs. Killed by a drone strike in Pakistan in 2008.

Abu Anas al-Libi (also known as Nazih Abdul-Hamed Nabih al-Ruqai'i): Under indictment for planning and conducting surveillance for the 1998 United States embassy bombings in Kenya and Tanzania.

Abu Faraj al-Libi (also known as Mustafa al-Uzayti): Considered the third-ranking figure in Al Qaeda until his arrest by Pakistani authorities in 2005.

Abu Salim prison: Maximum-security facility in Tripoli, Libya.

Abu Sufian bin Qumu (also known as Abdul Faris al-Libi): LIFG commander who was arrested by the Pakistanis, handed over to the United States, and extradited to Libya.

Abu Yahya al-Libi (also known as Mohamed Hassan Qaid): Libyan Islamist ideologue and propagandist who joined Al Qaeda and was killed by a CIA drone in 2012.

Ahmed Abu Khattala: Leader of Ansar al-Sharia.

Alawites: Followers of a branch of the Twelver school of Shi'a Islam. Predominantly located in Syria, with population also in the Golan Heights. President Assad is an Alawite.

Ali Zeidan: Former Libyan prime minister.

Al-Khaldan training camp: One of hundreds of Al Qaeda training camps in Afghanistan, established and run by members of Al Qaeda and the Taliban from 1996 to 2001. Founded by Ibn Al-Shaykh al-Libi.

Al-Muqatilah: "The fighting group," a powerful network of Libyan Afghans who brought jihad to Libya on the heels of the success of the mujahideen in Afghanistan in 1992.

Al-Naba TV: Qatari-funded television channel known as a local Al-Jazeera clone.

AQIM: Al Qaeda in the Islamic Maghreb.

Al-Sahab: Al Qaeda's propaganda arm.

Alwasat: Qatari-funded newspaper.

al-Watan party: Conservative Islamist political party in Libya, founded by Belhadj in November 2011 after the Libyan civil war and the overthrow of the Libyan Arab Jamahiriya.

Ammari Saifi: A leader of the Algerian Salafist Group for Preaching and Combat (SGPC).

Ansar al-Sharia Derna (ASD): Chapter of Ansar Al-Sharia founded by Bin Qumu.

Ansar al-Sharia in Benghazi (ASB): "Partisans of Islamic law," founded shortly after the end of the civil war by Muhammad al-Zahawi and unveiled publicly in February 2012.

Ansar al-Sharia in Yemen (ASY): Front established by Al Qaeda in the Arabian Peninsula (AQAP).

Ansar al-Sharia Tunisia (AST): Spinoff from derivatives of the February 17th Martyrs Brigade. It included former members of all of them and was led by Sufyan bin Qumu, a former Al Qaeda Guantanomo detainee.

Atiyah Abd al-Rahman: Libyan Islamist who joined Al Qaeda and who was killed by a drone in 2011.

Awad al-Zawawi: Islamist intellectual.

BMG: Blue Mountain Group, a Welsh security firm.

BML: Blue Mountain Libya, the Libyan branch of BMG.

Cherif Bassiouni: UN human rights investigator who led a team to Libya in summer 2011.

Chokri Belaid: Secular liberal Tunisian activist who was assassinated in February 2013.

Eclipse Group: Tripoli-based firm run by a Libyan–Jordanian who had good relationships with members of the nascent Libyan government and who partnered with BML.

Egyptian Muslim Brotherhood: Transnational Islamic organization founded in Egypt in 1928 and whose stated goal is to instill the Qur'an and Sunnah as the "sole reference point for . . . ordering the life of the Muslim family, individual, community . . . and state." In 2012, it became the first democratically elected political party in Egypt, but it is nevertheless considered a terrorist organization by the governments of Bahrain, Egypt, Russia, Syria, Saudi Arabia, and the United Arab Emirates.

Faraj al-Chalabi (also known as al-Shibli): LIFG coconspirator listed as a suspect in the planning of the Benghazi raid.

Fathi Terbil: A lawyer and the official spokesman for families of those killed in the 1996 Abu Salim massacre. His unlawful detention sparked protests.

Fawzi Bukatief: Muslim Brotherhood member who spent eighteen years in prison and who was a founder of the February 17th Martyrs Brigade.

Faylaka Island, Kuwait: Scene of a 2002 jihadist attack on two U.S. Marines in which one was killed, one wounded. Both attackers were killed.

February 17th Martyrs Brigade: Established by Ali al-Sallabi's brother Ismael, along with Fawzi Bukatief.

Guma El-Gamaty: UK coordinator for the new Libyan Interim National Council.

Harabi (Haribi): One of 140 Libyan tribes long at odds with Gaddafi.

I Go Aid: Relief organization that commissioned the vessel *Al Entisar* to transport humanitarian supplies (and likely weapons) from Benghazi to Misrata during the war.

Ibn al-Shaykh al-Libi (also known as Ali Mohamed al-Fakheri): Founder of Al-Khaldan Training Camp.

Ibrahim al-Jathran: Commander of the Petroleum Facilities Guard.

Imprisoned Omar Abdul Rahman Brigades: Militant salafi-jihadist group that emerged in 2012.

Islamic Front in Syria: Coalition of salafi-jihadist militias, some of which have explicit Al Qaeda ties.

Islamic Youth Shura Council of Darnah: Islamic extremist group established in March 2014 in Derna, Libya.

Ismael Ali Bakush: LIFG military committee member who trained many Al Qaeda operatives at a camp near Kabul, including a member who participated in the October 2002 attack against U.S. Marines on Faylaka Island, Kuwait.

Ismael al-Sallabi: Ali al Sallabi's brother, a founder of the February 17th Martyrs Brigade.

James R. Clapper: U.S. Director of National Intelligence.

Khalid al-Sharif (also known as Abu Hazem): LIFG commander arrested by the Pakistanis, handed over to the United States, and extradited to Libya.

Khalid al-Sharif: Former LIFG commander who reorganized some 10,000 militiamen into an official-sounding force dubbed the "National Guard."

King Mohammad Idris: Libya's first and only king, who reigned from 1951 to 1969. Chief of the Senussi Muslim order. Deposed in a 1969 coup d'etat launched by army officers led by Muammar Gaddafi while Idris was in Turkey for medical treatment.

Letfallah II: Ship carrying Libyan arms to Syria but intercepted and stopped in Lebanon.

Liwaa al-Umma: Militia force in Syria consisting of 6,000 fighters and founded by Harati.

Mahdi al-Harati: Commander of the Tripoli Brigades and deputy military commander of the TMC under Belhadj.

Major General Hamad Ben Ali al-Attiyah: Qatar's military chief of staff.

Majed Moqed: One of the 9/11 hijackers.

MANPADS: Man-portable air-defense systems.

Martyr Rafallah Sahati Brigade: Formed by Ismail al-Sallabi and Muhammad al-Gharabi after the war. Absorbed into Libya Shield in October 2012.

Miftah al-Dhawadi (also known as Abd-al-Ghaffar): The first emir of LIFG.

Mike Morell: Deputy director of the Central Intelligence Agency. Served as acting director twice, in 2011 and from 2012 to 2013.

MMRE: Malta to Misurata Relief Effort, a relief organization that commissioned the vessel *Al Entisar* to transport humanitarian supplies (and likely weapons) from Benghazi to Misrata during the war.

Mohammed Brahmi: Secular liberal Tunisian activist, assassinated in July 2013.

Moussa Koussa: Libyan intelligence chief.

Movement for Oneness and Jihad in West Africa (MOJWA): Splinter group of AQIM.

Muhammad al-Zahawi: Founder of Ansar al-Sharia in Benghazi.

Muhammad Jamal Network (MJN): Egyptian group closely affiliated with Al Qaeda and AQIM.

Mustafa al-Qunayfid (also known as Abu-al-Zubayr): A leading Al Muqatila military commander.

National Forces Alliance (NFA): Mahmoud Jibril's secularist coalition of fifty-eight parties formed in 2012 to counter the Muslim Brotherhood. Though considered liberal, the NFA advocated Sharia law and political Islam as a basis for government.

National Front for the Salvation of Libya: Political opposition group active in Libya during the years of the Gaddafi regime. Formed in 1981, it called for major liberalizing reforms.

Nawasi Brigade: Islamist militia in Tripoli led by Abdel-Raouf Al-Karah, operating under the aegis of the SSC.

Noman Benotman: Former LIFG leader.

Numeiri regime: The years 1969–1985 in Sudan, when President Gaafar Numeiri increasingly infused *sharia* into Sudanese civil law.

Petroleum Facilities Guard (PFG): 30,000-strong unit charged to protect oil installations in Libya.

Richard Reid: 2001 "shoe bomber."

Sadeq al-Ghariani: Grand mufti of the NTC from the time of the Libyan civil war to the present.

Sadiq al-Ghaithi (also known as Sadiq al-Obeidi): Former Libyan deputy defense minister. Sacked in January 2013, replaced by Khalid al-Sharif.

Saif al Islam Gaddafi: Political figure. The second son of Muammar Gaddafi.

Salafist Group for Preaching and Combat (SGPC): Previous name of AQIM.

Salah al-Barrani: Former LIFG fighter. Hasadi's field commander.

Sami al-Saadi (also known as Abu Munthir): LIFG spiritual leader.

Sanusiyya (the Senussi or Sanussi): Muslim political–religious Sufi order and tribe in Libya and the Sudan region, founded in Mecca in 1837. From 1902 to 1913, the Senussi fought French expansion in the Sahara, as well as the Italian colonization of Libya beginning in 1911. During World War I, the Senussi fought against the British in Egypt and Sudan. During World War II, the Senussi tribe provided vital support to the British 8th Army in north Africa against German and Italian forces. The Grand Senussi's grandson became King Idris of Libya in 1951. A third of the population in Libya is affiliated with the Senussi movement.

Satam al-Suqami: One of the 9/11 hijackers.

Seifallah ben Hassine (also known as Abu Iyad al-Tunisi): AST leader.

Serhane bin Abdelmajid Fakhet: One of the perpetrators in the March 2004 Madrid bombing. Arrested in Hong Kong and subsequently extradited to Libya.

Siham Sergewa: Libyan psychologist who claimed in May 2011 to have interviewed 295 Libyans raped at the hands of Gaddafi's regime.

Silvan Becker: German intelligence officer murdered, along with his wife, in Surt, Libya, in March 1994.

Tareq Muftah Durman: Associate of Belhadj.

Tayeb Oqaili: Representative of a Tunisian nongovernmental commission investigating the killings of Chokri Belaid and Mohammed Brahmi.

Umma al-Wasat Party: Rigidly Islamist party founded by Saadi and Qaid.

Wisam bin Hamid (also known as bin Ahmed): Reputed Iraq war veteran, militant Islamist, and prominent Libyan Shield commander.

Yusuf Qaradawi: Leading theologian of the Muslim Brotherhood.

Notes

An index of linked footnote references can be found at
http://www.architectsofdisaster.com/footnotes/.

1. In a June 15, 2011, report to Congress, the administration acknowledged that ending U.S. participation in the NATO campaign "would likely lead to the withdrawal of other NATO and coalition nation participation in the operation." See "United States Activities in Libya," White House report to Congress, June 15, 2011.

2. Judith Miller, "How Gadhafi Lost His Groove," Wall Street Journal, May 16, 2006.

3. Ibid.

4. Andy Bloxham and Damien McElroy, "Moussa Koussa, a High-Profile Lockerbie Spymaster," The Telegraph, March 30, 2011.

5. Duncan Gardham and Christopher Hope, "Libya: Moussa Koussa, the Intelligence Chief Who Was an Enemy of the West and Then Its Friend," The Telegraph, March 31, 2011.

6. LCDR Joseph T. Stanik, USN (Ret.), "HH 362—History of the Middle East," U.S. Naval Academy, April 2002.

7. "Chronology of Libya's Disarmament and Relations with the United States," Arms Control Association, February 2014.

8. "U.S. Says Libya Implementing WMD Pledge," Arms Control Association.

9. Ibid.

10. "Chronology of Libya's Disarmament and Relations with the United States," Arms Control Association, February 2014.

11. Associated Press, "Libya Steadily Inches from Adversary to Ally," Tampa Bay Times, January 4, 2008.

12. "US Moves Closer to Libya despite Lingering Concerns," The Jerusalem Post, January 4, 2008.

13. "U.S. Says Libya Implementing WMD Pledge," Arms Control Association.

14. Ken Silverstein, "How Kadafi Went from Foe to Ally," Los Angeles Times, September 4, 2005.

15. "Libya: Progress on the Path toward Cautious Reengagement," Hearing of the House Committee on International Relations, March 16, 2005.

16. "Libya Gives Mali 2 Security Planes," News24, April 10, 2010.

17. Omar Deghayes, Abdul Ra'ouf al-Qassim (identified as Abdul Rauf Al Qusin in some Pentagon documents), and Omar Khalifh, "Guantánamo Inmate Tells of Libyan Death Threat," The Guardian (London), February 16, 2005. "Foreign Interrogators in Guantanamo Bay," Center for Constitutional Rights.

18. See "Delivered into Enemy Hands: US-Led Abuse and Rendition of Opponents to Gaddafi's Libya," Human Rights Watch, September 2012.

19. Ken Silverstein, "How Kadafi Went from Foe to Ally," *Los Angeles Times*, September 4, 2005.

20. "Libya: Words to Deeds," Human Rights Watch, January 2006.

21. "Transcript: Obama's Full Interview with NPR," National Public Radio, June 1, 2009.

22. Associated Press, "Obama Seeks 'New Beginning' in Muslim World," NBC News, June 4, 2009.

23. Charles Crawford, "That Obama 2009 Cairo Speech—in Retrospect," Pundit-Wire, July 8, 2013.

24. "Hillary's war: How conviction replaced skepticism in Libya intervention," *Washington Post*, October 30, 2011.

25. Raymond Ibrahim, "How Taqiyya Alters Islam's Rules of War," *Middle East Quarterly*, winter 2010.

26. Ibid.

27. "Taqqiya—An Tactic of Lying, Concealment," The Clarion Project, April 7, 2014.

28. "Remarks by the President at the National Defense University," Office of the Press Secretary, The White House, May 23, 2013.

29. David Remnick, "Going the Distance: On and Off the Road with Barack Obama," *The New Yorker*, January 27, 2014.

30. "US Policy Change: Negotiate with Terrorists; Obama Seeks Direct Talks with Taliban," Before It's News. Rob Crilly, "US Seeks Direct Talks with Taliban's Mullah Omar," *The Telegraph*, Telegraph Media Group, June 5, 2011.

31. David Remnick, "Going the Distance: On and Off the Road with Barack Obama," *The New Yorker*, January 27, 2014.

32. "Remarks of John O. Brennan, Assistant to the President for Homeland Security and Counterterrorism, on Ensuring al-Qa'ida's Demise—As Prepared for Delivery," Office of the Press Secretary, The White House, June 29, 2011.

33. "Red Teaming and Alternative Analysis," Red Team Journal.

34. "Hillary's war: How conviction replaced skepticism in Libya intervention," *Washington Post*, October 30, 2011.

35. "Security Council Approves 'No-Fly Zone' over Libya, Authorizing 'All Necessary Measures' to Protect Civilians, by Vote of 10 in Favour with 5 Abstentions," United Nations Security Council, March 17, 2011.

36. Michael Birnbaum and Joby Warrick, "NATO Steps Up Bombing in Libya; Rebels Report Gains," *Washington Post*, May 10, 2011.

37. "Remarks by the President in Address to the Nation on Libya, National Defense University, Washington, D.C.," March 28, 2011. Michael Birnbaum

and Joby Warrick, "NATO Steps up Bombing in Libya," *Washington Post*, May 10, 2011.

38. Laura Rozen, "Averting 'Srebrenica on Steroids': White House Defends Libya Operations," Yahoo! News, March 23, 2011.

39. "Libya: Ten Things about Gaddafi They Don't Want You to Know," Global Research, November 16, 2014.

40. Two months into the war, Italian Foreign Minister Franco Frattini said that 10,000 had died. "Libya Rebels Say 10,000 Killed, UN Sends in Food Aid," Agence France-Presse, April 19, 2011. "We were looking at 'Srebrenica on steroids'—the real or imminent possibility that up to 100,000 people could be massacred, and everyone would blame us for it," said White House Middle East strategist Dennis Ross. See Laura Rozen, "Averting 'Srebrenica on Steroids': White House Defends Libya Operations," Yahoo! News, March 23, 2011. Ambassador to Libya Gene Cretz noted that U.S. officials have seen figures ranging from 10,000 to 30,000. See Bradley Klapper, "Libya Death Toll Could Be as High as 30,000: U.S.," The World Post, April 27, 2011.

41. Ian Black, "Libyan Revolution Casualties Lower Than Expected, Says New Government," *The Guardian*, January 8, 2013; "Libya: Estimate of Revolution Casualties Lowered," *The Guardian* (London), January 9, 2013.

42. "There are grounds for questioning the more sensational reports that the regime was using its air force to slaughter demonstrators." The ICG interviewed two senior Western journalists upon their return from Libya, both of whom said that "none of their Libyan interlocutors in Benghazi or other towns under the opposition's control had made any mention of the regime's supposed use of airpower against unarmed demonstrators in the first few days of the protests." International Crisis Group, "Popular Protest in North Africa and the Middle East (V): Making Sense of Libya," June 6, 2011, pp. 4–5.

43. "Sexual Violence in Libya, the Middle East and North Africa," Press Statement, Hillary Rodham Clinton, Secretary of State, June 16, 2011.

44. Ewen MacAskill, "Gaddafi 'Supplies Troops with Viagra to Encourage Mass Rape,' Claims Diplomat," *The Guardian*, April 30, 2011.

45. Sara Sidner and Amir Ahmed, "Psychologist: Proof of Hundreds of Rape Cases during Libya's War," CNN, May 23, 2011.

46. Kareem Fahim, "Claims of Wartime Rapes Unsettle and Divide Libyans," *New York Times*, June 20, 2011.

47. HRW said that it "could not confirm claims of mass or systematic rape" by Gaddafi's forces. See "Libya: Transitional Government Should Support Victims," Human Rights Watch, September 19, 2011.

48. Amnesty International, "The Battle for Libya: Killings, Disappearances and Torture," September 13, 2011, MDE 19/025/2011.

49. "Popular Protest in North Africa and the Middle East (V): Making Sense of Libya," Middle East/North Africa Report N°107 June 6, 2011.

50. Agence France-Presse, "UN Official, Investigator at Odds over Libya Mass Rape Claim," June 10, 2001.

51. See, for example, Peter Finn, "Experts Say Gaddafi Relying on Paramilitary Forces, Foreign Mercenaries to Crush Protests," *Washington Post*, February 24, 2011. Nabila Ramdani, "Libya Protests: 'Foreign Mercenaries Using Heavy Weapons against Demonstrators,'" *The Telegraph* (London), February 20, 2011. Abigail Hauslohner, "Libyan Leader's Delusions of African Grandeur," *Time*, February 22, 2011. Scott Baldauf, "Qaddafi's Ties to Rebel Groups Scrutinized as 'African Mercenaries' Patrol Libya," *Christian Science Monitor*, February 23, 2011.

52. "Secretary Clinton Addresses United Nations Human Rights Council," U.S. Department of State, February 28, 2011.

53. "Libya and Africa: Pogrom," *The Economist*, October 12, 2000.

54. Korva Coleman, "Gadhafi Using Foreign Children as Mercenaries in Libya," NPR, March 3, 2011.

55. In a March 2, 2011, interview with Radio Netherlands Worldwide, Peter Bouckaert of Human Rights Watch said that he had found no proof of mercenaries' being used by the regime after two weeks in Libya. Some 156 alleged mercenaries then under detention in Benghazi were, according to Bouckaert, Libyan citizens of sub-Saharan African descent. See "HRW: No Mercenaries in Eastern Libya," Radio Netherlands Worldwide, March 2, 2011.

56. After a lengthy investigation, Amnesty International concluded that the "allegations about the use of mercenaries proved to be largely unfounded." See "Libya: The Battle for Libya: Killings, Disappearances and Torture," Amnesty International, September 2011, p. 83.

57. "Libya: Col Gaddafi 'Has Spent £2.1M on Mercenaries,'" *The Telegraph*, April 20, 2011.

58. "Libya: Gaddafi on the 'Back Foot,' Says Liam Fox," BBC, April 27, 2011.

59. In his March 28 address to the nation, Obama said that "broadening our military mission to include regime change would be a mistake." See "Remarks by the President in Address to the Nation on Libya, National Defense University, Washington, D.C.," March 28, 2011.

60. Patricia Zengerle, "Obama Hopes Gaddafi Will Ultimately Step Down," Reuters, March 29, 2011.

61. Joby Warrick, "Hillary's war: How conviction replaced skepticism in Libya intervention," *Washington Post*, October 30, 2011.

62. Adam Entous, Keith Johnson, and Charles Levinson, "Amid Libya Rebels, 'Flickers' of alQaeda," *Wall Street Journal*, March 30, 2011.

63. "United States Activities in Libya," White House report to Congress, June 15, 2011.

64. Omar Ashour, "Libya's Muslim Brotherhood Faces the Future," The Brookings Institution, March 9, 2012.

65. Mahan Abedin, "From Mujahid to Activist: An Interview with a Libyan Veteran of the Afghan Jihad," Spotlight on Terror (Jamestown Foundation), March 24, 2005.

66. *Al-Hayat* (London), October 20, 1995; Gary Gambill; "The Libyan Islamic Fighting Group (LIFG)," *Terrorism Monitor*, March 24, 2005.

67. Paul Cruickshank. Susan Candiotti, and Tim Lister, "Sources: Benghazi Suspect Detained in Libya," CNN, March 14, 2013.

68. Mahan Abedin, "From Mujahid to Activist: An Interview with a Libyan Veteran of the Afghan Jihad," Spotlight on Terror (Jamestown Foundation), March 24, 2005.

69. See "The Shayler Affair: The Spooks, the Colonel and the Jailed Whistle-Blower," The Observer (London), August 9, 1998.

70. "Senior Bin Laden Aide Is Arrested in Sudan," The Independent (London), March 20, 2002. Duncan Gardham, "CIA 'Used Manchester Manual to Justify Water Boarding,'" The Telegraph (London), October 28, 2011. John Rosenthal, "Is Libi's Al-Qaeda Manual a Blueprint for Arab Spring?" Al-Monitor, October 20, 2013.

71. ABC (Madrid), September 5, 2011, and September 9, 2011.

72. "Libyan Man Jailed in Britain for Having 'Terror Documents': Police," Agence France-Presse, July 17, 2007. Contemporaneous news accounts list the defendant's name as Al-Bashir Mohammed al-Faqih, an alias listed for Abd al-Rahman al-Faqih in the Treasury Department's designation (it is not entirely clear which name is correct).

73. Abd al-Rahman al-Faqih (QI.A.212.06), "UN Security Council Committee pursuant to Resolutions 1267 (1999) and 1989 (2011) concerning Al-Qaida and Associated Individuals and Entities," August 13, 2009. According to the U.S. Treasury Department, the LIFG as an organization "is believed to have participated in the planning of the May 2003 Casablanca suicide bombings," suggesting that there is further evidence of LIFG involvement that remains classified. See "Three LIFG Members Designation for Terrorism," U.S. Department of the Treasury, October 30, 2008.

74. Joseph Felter and Brian Fishman, "Al-Qa'ida's Foreign Fighters in Iraq: A First Look at the Sinjar Records," Combating Terrorism Center, U.S. Military Academy, West Point, NY, December 2007, pp. 7–9.

75. Felter and Fishman, op cit., pp. 10–12.

76. For example, Mauritanian national Akhmed Aziz (also known as Ahmed Ould AbdelAziz) detailed his stays at several LIFG bases and guesthouses in Afghanistan and Pakistan. See "JTF-GTMO Detainee Assessment: Ahmed Ould Abdel Aziz," February 27, 2008.

77. "Die Hard in Derna," U.S. Embassy Tripoli, Reference ID 08TRIPOLI430, June 2, 2008.

78. "At Least 10 Die in Libya Riot over Caricatures," Los Angeles Times, February 18, 2006.

79. Al-Sharq al-Awsat (London), "Libya to Demolish Notorious Abu-Salim Prison," September 10, 2009.

80. M. Khayat, "The Salafi-Jihadi Challenge in Libya, Part II: The Role of the LIFG and Its Former Commander 'Abd Al-Hakim Belhadj," MEMRI, August 26, 2011.

81. Tim Lister and Paul Cruickshank, "Exclusive: Senior Al Qaeda Figure 'Living in Libyan Capital,'" CNN, September 27, 2012.

82. "When America invades a country, the insurgency is legal and lawful. From a religious point of view, it is permissible and we have to support it," said Sadeq. "Violence against occupation is a sacred act . . . a sacred jihad," concurred Ali al-Salabi. See "Former Militants Wage a New Battlein Native Libya," *Washington Post*, May 31, 2010.

83. "I don't believe bin Laden is calling for the killing of any single civilian," Saadi told the *Washington Post*. See Sudarsan Raghavan, "Former Militants Wage a New Battle in Native Libya," *Washington Post*, May 31, 2010.

84. "Libyan Police Stations Torched," Al-Jazeera, February 16, 2011.

85. *Al-Hayat* (London), February 17, 2011. Libya released 110 Islamists of the Al-Qaeda-linked Libyan Islamic Fighting Group (LIFG), an AFP correspondent witnessed. See "AFP: Clashes Erupt as Libya Braces for 'Day of Anger,'" Agence France-Presse, February 16, 2011.

86. Justin Fishel and Jennifer Griffin, "Sources: Former Guantanamo Detainees Suspected of Joining ISIS, Other Groups in Syria," Fox News, October 30, 2014.

87. "Libyan Police Stations Torched," Al-Jazeera, February 16, 2011.

88. Charles Levinson, "Ex-Mujahedeen Help Lead Libyan Rebels," *Wall Street Journal*, April 2, 2011.

89. Graeme Smith, "A Rebellion Divided: Spectre of Revenge Killings Hangs over Eastern Libya," *The Globe and Mail* (Toronto), April 1, 2011.

90. "In East Libya, Kadhafi Foes See End of Regime," Agence France-Presse, February 23, 2011.

91. Al-Jazeera satellite TV (Doha), February 25, 2011.

92. "JTF-GTMO Detainee Assessment: Abu Sufian Ibrahim Ahmed Hamuda Bin Qumu," April 22, 2005.

93. David D. Kirkpatrick, "The New Islamists: Libya Democracy Clashes with Fervor for Jihad," *New York Times*, June 24, 2012.

94. For an English translation of the interview, see "NATO Helps Former Mujahid Come to Power in Libya," *Al-Monitor*, January 25, 2012.

95. Hadeel Al-Shalchi and Maggie Michael, "Libya Rebel Commander Plays Down Islamist Past," Yahoo! News, September 2, 2011.

96. "El comandante rebelde Belhadj admite que contactó con los cabecillas del 11-M," ABC (Madrid), September 10, 2011.

97. David D. Kirkpatrick and Rod Nordland, "Tripoli Divided as Rebels Jostle to Fill Power Vacuum," *New York Times*, August 31, 2011.

98. "I was captured in 2002 in Peshawar, Pakistan, on my way back from Afghanistan where I fought against foreign invasion. I was handed over to the Americans, held a few months in Islamabad delivered to Libya, and released in 2008." See "Reportage. 'Noi ribelli, islamici e tolleranti,'" *Il Sole 24 Ore*, March 22, 2011.

99. "Reportage. 'Noi ribelli, islamici e tolleranti,'" *Il Sole 24 Ore*, March 22, 2011.

100. Graeme Smith, "Rebels Stand apart from Extremists," *The Globe and Mail* (Toronto), March 12, 2011, A19.

101. "Libya: Defining U.S. Security Interests," Hearing of the House Foreign Affairs Committee, March 31, 2011.

102. Charles Levinson, "Ex-Mujahedeen Help Lead Libyan Rebels," *Wall Street Journal*, April 2, 2011.

103. "Last Air Mission of Unified Protector Concluded," NATO, October 31, 2011.

104. Sam Dagher, Charles Levinson, and Margaret Coker, "Tiny Kingdom's Huge Role in Libya Draws Concern," *Wall Street Journal*, October 17, 2001.

105. "The numbers of Qataris on the ground were hundreds in every region," Qatari chief of staff Major Geneneral Hamad Ben Ali al-Attiyah later acknowledged. See "Qatar Admits It Had Boots on Ground in Libya," Agence France-Presse, October 26, 2011.

106. "Qatar Admits It Had Boots on Ground in Libya," Agence France-Presse, October 26, 2011.

107. "Power Brokers—Qatar and the UAE Take Centre Stage," *Jane's Intelligence Review*, January 1, 2012.

108. Sam Dagher, Charles Levinson, and Margaret Coker, "Tiny Kingdom's Huge Role in Libya Draws Concern," *Wall Street Journal*, October 17, 2001.

109. David D. Kirkpatrick and Rod Nordland, "Tripoli Divided as Rebels Jostle to Fill Power Vacuum," *New York Times*, August 31, 2011.

110. Omar Ashour, "Libya's Muslim Brotherhood Faces the Future," The Brookings Institution, March 9, 2012.

111. Harriet Sherwood and Xan Rice, "Muammar Gaddafi Calls for Ceasefire in Libyan TV Address," *The Guardian*, April 30, 2011.

112. "Statement on Libya," NATO, April 14, 2011.

113. Omar Ashour, "Libyan Islamists Unpacked: Rise, Transformation, and Future," Brookings Doha Center, May 2012.

114. Sharyl Attkisson, "Thousands of Libyan Missiles from Qaddafi Era Missing in Action," CBS News, March 25, 2013.

115. Marshall Curtis Erwin, "Sensitive Covert Action Notifications: Oversight Options for Congress," Congressional Research Service, April 10, 2013.

116. David Samuels, "A Conversation with Colin Powell," *The Atlantic*, April 2007.

117. "Al-Qaeda in Libya: A Profile," Federal Research Division, Library of Congress, August 2012, pp. 7, 15.

118. According to John Rosenthal, Hamid was quoted by Islamist websites as saying in October 2011 that sharia (Islamic law) "is a red line" and "we will not cede one rule of it." See John Rosenthal, "Benghazi: Marines 'Supported' by Jihadists," WorldNetDaily, October 16, 2012.

119. "Extremists Threaten Mutilation and Death for Seized 'Homosexuals,'" *Libya Herald*, November 26, 2012.

120. "Libya Islamists Destroy Sufi Shrines, Library: Military," Reuters, August 25, 2012.

121. Frederic Wehrey, "The Wrath of Libya's Salafis," Carnegie Endowment for International Peace, September 12, 2012.

122. George Grant and Mohamed Bujenah, "Update II: Security Forces Arrest Man in Connection with Benghazi Killings, Four Policemen Killed in Failed Release Attempt," Libya Herald, December 16, 2012.

123. "Mixed Signals: Libya Struggles to Deal with Eastern Militias," Jane's Intelligence Review, February 1, 2014.

124. Frederic Wehrey, "The Wrath of Libya's Salafis," Carnegie Endowment for International Peace, September 12, 2012. Anas El Gomati, "In Libya, Militias Rule," Al-Monitor, June 18, 2013.

125. Ryszard Bouvier, "Fashloum Youth Demand Government Action against Nawasi Brigade; Others Support It," Libya Herald, January 12, 2013.

126. Frederic Wehrey, "Libya Doesn't Need More Militias," New York Times, June 10, 2013.

127. Jason Pack and Barak Barfi, "In War's Wake: The Struggle for Post-Qadhafi Libya," Policy

Focus No. 118, Washington Institute for Near East Policy, February 2012. Abdel Hakim Belhaj, "The Revolution Belongs to All Libyans, Secular or Not," The Guardian, September 27, 2011.

128. "It was Belhadj who handled the training of Ansar al-Sharia in Tunisia, including the cell that would go on to assassinate Belaid and Brahmi," said Oqaili. See Noureddine Baltayeb, "Tunisia: New Details in Opposition Assassination Point to Libyan Islamist," Al-Akhbar (English), October 3, 2013. Echorouk Online, an influential Algerian news website, reported on February 18, 2013, "The Islamic Fighting Group's leader in Libya and the Tripoli Military Council's commander Abdelhakim Belhadj is not allowed to enter Algeria as he is suspected of being involved in terrorist acts."

129. Wolfram Lacher, "Fault Lines of the Revolution: Political Actors, Camps, and Conflicts," German Institute for International Security and Affairs, May 2013.

130. Jathran and several of his brothers organized an armed cell in Ajdabiya that was broken up by the authorities in 2005. After their release from prison during the first week of the 2011 uprising (alongside others who were almost exclusively LIFG members), they acknowledged having recruited Libyans to fight in Iraq but insisted that only "two or three" members of their cell were LIFG members. See Evan Hill, "One Family against Gaddafi," Al-Jazeera, March 18, 2011.

131. "Libya Oil Deadlock Causes Jitters in Global Energy Market," UPI, December 18, 2013.

132. "Black Boxes Found from Libyan Plane Crash in Tunisia," Agence France-Presse, February 22, 2014.

133. "A Local Al Jazeera Clone," Maghreb Confidential, August 29, 2013.

134. "Sharia Law Declaration Raises Concerns in New Libya," Agence France-Presse, October 24, 2011.

135. Mary Beth Sheridan, "Libya Declares Liberation with an Islamic Tone," *Washington Post*, October 23, 2011.

136. Dominique Soguel, "Ghariani Embodies Image of Muslim Libya in Post-Gathafi Era," Middle East Online, April 16, 2012.

137. Jamie Dettmer, "Libya's Grand Mufti: Teachers Must Veil," *The Daily Beast*, October 24, 2013.

138. Dominique Soguel, "Ghariani Embodies Image of Muslim Libya in Post-Gathafi Era," Middle East Online, April 16, 2012.

139. Ibid.

140. Susan Jones, "Libya's Grand Mufti Issues Fatwa against U.N. Report on Women's Rights," CNSNews, March 12, 2013.

141. Patrick Sawer, "Radical Cleric Uses UK as Base to Preach in Support of Violent Islamists," *The Telegraph*, August 30, 2014.

142. Ashraf Abdul Wahab, "Grand Mufti Calls for Changes to School Textbooks," *Libya Herald*, October 18, 2012.

143. Chris Stephen and Josh Halliday, "UK Accused of Harbouring Libyan Cleric Who Helped Aid Islamist Insurgency," *The Guardian*, August 29, 2014.

144. Patrick Sawer, "Radical Cleric Uses UK as Base to Preach in Support of Violent Islamists," *The Telegraph*, August 30, 2014.

145. Stephen F. Hayes and Thomas Joscelyn, "Questions They Won't Answer: Benghazi Isn't Going Away," *Weekly Standard*, November 11, 2013.

146. Julian Pecquet, "Hillary: Benghazi 'My Biggest Regret,'" *The Hill*, January 27, 2014.

147. Stevens personally introduced NTC leader Mahmoud Jibril to Secretary of State Clinton in Paris in March 2011. See "US Gauges Libyan Opposition in Paris as Allies Call for Swift Military Intervention," *Washington Post*, March 14, 2011.

148. "Scenesetter for Secretary Rice's Visit to Libya," Cable 08TRIPOLI680_a, U.S. Embassy, Tripoli, August 29, 2008.

149. David D. Kirkpatrick, "A Deadly Mix in Benghazi," *New York Times*, December 28, 2013.

150. Robin Wright, "What Ambassador Chris Stevens Would Have Wanted Us to Do in the Middle East," *Washington Post*, September 14, 2012.

151. Untitled, U.S. State Department, December 17, 2012, pp. 14–15, 30.

152. A December 2011 memo by Assistant Secretary for Near Eastern Affairs Jeffrey Feltman, who visited Benghazi the preceding May and August, noted, "Many Libyans have said the U.S. presence in Benghazi has a salutary, calming effect on easterners who are fearful that the new focus on Tripoli could once again lead to their neglect and exclusion from reconstruction and wealth distribution and strongly favor a permanent U.S. presence in the form of a full consulate." See "Action Memo for Under Secretary Kennedy," U.S. Department of State, December 27, 2011, Mark Hosenball and Susan Cornwell, "U.S. Intended to Keep Benghazi Mission Open through 2012," Reuters, October 19, 2012.

153. Mark Hosenball, "U.S. Intelligence Set Back When Libya Base Was Abandoned," Reuters, October 12, 2012.

154. Adam Entous, Siobhan Gorman, and Margaret Coker, "CIA Takes Heat for Role in Libya," *Wall Street Journal*, November 1, 2012.

155. "U.S. Officials: CIA Ran Benghazi Consulate," UPI, November 2, 2012.

156. "Analysis: CIA Role in Benghazi Underreported," CNN, May 15, 2013.

157. Margaret Coker, Adam Entous, Jay Solomon, and Siobhan Gorman, "Miscues before Libya Assault," *Wall Street Journal*, September 21, 2012.

158. Adam Entous, Siobhan Gorman, Margaret Coker, "CIA Takes Heat for Role in Libya," *Wall Street Journal*, November 1, 2012.

159. "Review of the Terrorist Attacks on U.S. Facilities in Benghazi, Libya, September 11–12, 2012," U.S. Senate Select Committee on Intelligence, January 15, 2014, pp. 27–28.

160. Jennifer Griffin and Adam Housley, "Exclusive: Petraeus Mistress May Have Revealed Classified Information at Denver Speech on Real Reason for Libya Attack," Fox News, November 12, 2012.

161. Eric Schmitt, "C.I.A. Said to Aid in Steering Arms to Syrian Opposition," *New York Times*, June 21, 2102.

162. "Exclusive: Dozens of CIA Operatives on the Ground during Benghazi Attack," CNN, August 1, 2013.

163. "Security Incidents since 2011," Regional Security Office, U.S. Embassy, Tripoli, Libya.

164. Untitled U.S. State Department, December 17, 2012, pp. 14–15, 30; "Security Incidents since 2011."

165. "The Security Failures of Benghazi," hearing before the U.S. House Committee on Oversight and Government Reform, October 10, 2012.

166. Email from Deputy Assistant Secretary for Diplomatic Security Charlene Lamb to Principal Deputy Assistant Secretary for Diplomatic Security Scott Bultrowicz, with carbon copies to Assistant Secretary of State for Diplomatic Security Eric Boswell and Deputy Assistant Secretary of State for Countermeasures Gentry Smith, "Re: British Motorcade Attacked in Benghazi, June 11, 2012," cited in "Benghazi: Where Is the State Department Accountability?" Majority Staff Report, House Foreign Affairs Committee, February 7, 2014.

167. "U.S. Memo Warned of High Risk of Libya Violence," CBS News, October 18, 2012.

168. Travel Warning, U.S. Department of State, Bureau of Consular Affairs, "Libya," August 27, 2012.

169. Senate Select Committee on Intelligence, op. cit., p. 9.

170. Defense Intelligence Agency, "Libya: Terrorists Now Targeting U.S. and Western Interests," June 12, 2012, cited in House Permanent Select Committee on Intelligence "Review of the Terrorist Attacks on U.S. Facilities

in Benghazi, Libya," September 11–12, 2012, U.S. Senate Select Committee on Intelligence, January 15, 2014, p. 9.

171. Pentagon Joint Staff, "Terrorism: Conditions Ripe for More Attacks, Terrorist Safe Haven in Libya," J-2 Intelligence Update, June 18, 2012, cited in House Permanent Select Committee on Intelligence "Review of the Terrorist Attacks on U.S. Facilities in Benghazi, Libya," September 11–12, 2012, U.S. Senate Select Committee on Intelligence, January 15, 2014, p. 9.

172. Pentagon Joint Staff, "Libya: Terrorists to Increase Strength during Next Six Months," J-2 Intelligence Update, August 19, 2012, cited in "Review of the Terrorist Attacks on U.S. Facilities in Benghazi, Libya," September 11–12, 2012, U.S. Senate Select Committee on Intelligence, January 15, 2014, p. 9.

173. Testimony of Lieutenant Colonel Andrew Wood before the House Committee on Oversight and Government Reform, October 10, 2012.

174. The SSCI report noted a "significant difference in security staffing between the two facilities. In September 2012, there were three Diplomatic Security agents assigned to the Temporary Mission Facility, while there were nine security officers out of a total of II individuals at the CIA Annex . . . . In sum, the Mission facility had a much weaker security posture than the Annex, with a significant disparity in the quality." See House Permanent Select Committe on Intelligence "Review of the Terrorist Attacks on U.S. Facilities in Benghazi, Libya," September 11–12, 2012, U.S. Senate Select Committee on Intelligence, January 15, 2014, p. 19.

175. "That's fine," he continued, "but no one's ever come out and said that, that we made that risk and we made that decision, and then take responsibility for it." See "Benghazi: Exposing Failure and Recognizing Courage," hearing before the U.S. House Committee on Oversight and Government Reform, May 8, 2013.

176. "Action Memo for Under Secretary Kennedy," U.S. Department of State, December 27, 2011.

177. Senate Select Committee on Intelligence, op. cit., pp. 14–15, 30.

178. "Benghazi: Exposing Failure and Recognizing Courage," hearing before the House Committee on Oversight and Government Reform, May 8, 2013.

179. Shane Harris, "Chris Stevens' Benghazi Diary Reveals His Brooding, Hopeful Final Days," Foreign Policy, June 26, 2013.

180. Ibid.

181. Catherine Herridge and Pamela Browne, "Was Syrian Weapons Shipment Factor in Ambassador's Benghazi Visit?" Fox News, October 25, 2012. A September 11 meeting with Mohammad al-Mufti, head of the al-Marfta Shipping Company, may have been related.

182. Paul Schemm and Maggie Michael, "Libyan Witnesses Recount Organized Benghazi Attack," Associated Press, October 27, 2012.

183. Senate Select Committee on Intelligence, op. cit., pp. 14–15, 30.

184. Background Briefing on Libya, U.S. Department of State, October 9, 2012.

185. Senate Select Committee on Intelligence, op. cit., pp. 35–36.

186. Senate Select Committee on Intelligence, op. cit., pp. 14–15, 30.

187. 17 Translation: "The martyrs of February 17 battalion absolutely denies any confrontation between [February 17] and the youth that invaded the embassy."

188. Senate Select Committee on Intelligence, op. cit., p. 36.

189. Report of the Benghazi Accountability Review Board, U.S. State Department, December 17, 2012, p. 5.

190. "Sensitive Documents Left with Little Security at U.S. mission in Benghazi," *Washington Post*, October 3, 2012.

191. "Benghazi: Exposing Failure and Recognizing Courage," hearing before the House Committee on Oversight and Government Reform, May 8, 2013.

192. "Libyan Guards' Eyewitness Accounts from Inside Benghazi U.S. Consulate during September 11 Attack Suggest Attack Was Well-Planned, American and Libyan Response Was Lacking," The Middle East Media Research Institute, Special Dispatch No. 4995, October 8, 2012.

193. Kelly McParland, "Bungling and Comically Inadequate Security Produced the Tragedy in Benghazi," *National Post*, December 19, 2012.

194. Senate Select Committee on Intelligence, op. cit.

195. Matt Smith, "Ex-SEALs, Online Gaming Maven among Benghazi Dead," CNN, September 13, 2012.

196. David D. Kirkpatrick, "A Deadly Mix in Benghazi," *New York Times*, December 28, 2013.

197. Diana West, "Meet Wissam bin Hamid, Uncle Sam's Jihadist Security Officer," October 24, 2012.

198. Senate Select Committee on Intelligence, op. cit., p. 35.

199. "Benghazi: Exposing Failure and Recognizing Courage," hearing before the House Committee on Oversight and Government Reform, May 8, 2013.

200. "October 11, 2012 Debate Transcript."

201. Testimony of Secretary Hillary Clinton before the House Foreign Affairs Committee on January 23, 2013.

202. "Benghazi: Where Is the State Department Accountability?" Majority Staff Report, House Foreign Affairs Committee, February 7, 2014, p. 13.

203. Oren Dorell, "State: No One Fired over Benghazi Attack," *USA Today*, August 20, 2013.

204. Senate Select Committee on Intelligence, op. cit., p. 6.

205. Jan Stevens, "Carry on His Good Work," CNN, June 26, 2013.

206. Senate Select Committee on Intelligence, op. cit., p. 3.

207. "Libyan President el-Megarif Reportedly Eyes Al Qaeda in 'Preplanned' Attack on US Consulate," Fox News, September 16, 2012.

208. "Consulate Attack Preplanned, Libya's President Says," National Public Radio, September 16, 2012. Other Libyan officials disagreed. The deputy interior minister with responsibility for the east of Libya, Wanis Al-Sharif, blamed both Qaddafi elements and US security personnel, who he said had provoked the attack by shooting at peaceful demonstrators. See Nihal Zaroug and MahaEllawati, "US Consulate Attack 'Pre-Planned' Says Magarief," *Libya Herald*, September 14, 2012.

209. "Libya Identifies 50 Involved in U.S. Attack: Official," Reuters, September 15, 2012.

210. Eli Lake, "Obama's Shaky Libya Narrative," *The Daily Beast*, September 21, 2012.

211. Kevin F. Kolbye, Dallas FBI's Assistant Special Agent in Charge, was On-Scene Commander for the investigation and claimed at a GovSec West Conference in Dallas (though he was never called to testify before Congress) that FBI officials were in Benghazi within two days of the attack, despite news reports' saying that the FBI did not arrive until weeks later. See Jamie Friedlander, "FBI Special Agent Discusses Counterterrorism at GovSec West 2013," Security Today, November 21, 2013. Kerry Picket, "Lead FBI Benghazi Investigator Has Never Testified before Congress," Breitbart.com, December 9, 2013.

212. Eileen Sullivan and Lolita C. Baldor, "FBI Came to Benghazi and Left in Past 24 Hours," Associated Press, October 4, 2012.

213. Richard Esposito, Jonathan Dienst, and Joe Valiquette, "FBI Seeks Help Identifying Three Suspects Seen at Benghazi Mission during Attack," NBC News, May 1, 2013.

214. "Information Sought on Attacks in Benghazi," FBI, May 2013.

215. "Seeking Information on Benghazi Attacks," FBI.

216. The FBI page states: "We need your help to solve this crime. If you have any information, text or e-mail BenghaziTips@ic.fbi.gov or submit information confidentially at https://forms.fbi.gov/benghazi-en."

217. Ted Barrett, "U.S. Identifies Some Involved in Benghazi Attack, Lawmaker Says," CNN, May 21, 2013.

218. Catherine Herridge, "Lawmakers Question Why Benghazi Suspects Missing from 'Rewards for Justice' Program," Fox News, October 29, 2013.

219. Senate Select Committee on Intelligence, op. cit., p. 41.

220. Bill Gertz, "Benghazi Attack Suspect Walks," *Washington Free Beacon*, June 27, 2013.

221. Ibid.

222. Senate Select Committee on Intelligence, op. cit., p. 41.

223. Ibid.

224. Devlin Barrett, "U.S. Files Charges in Benghazi Attack," *Wall Street Journal*, August 6, 2013.

225. Evan Perez, "First Criminal Charges Filed in Benghazi Attack Probe," CNN, August 7, 2013.

226. David D. Kirkpatrick, "Suspect in Libya Attack, in Plain Sight, Scoffs at U.S.," New York Times, October 18, 2012.

227. Evan Perez, "First Criminal Charges Filed in Benghazi Attack Probe," CNN, August 7, 2013

2013. John King and Chelsea J. Carter, "Lawmaker: If CNN Can Interview Suspect in Benghazi Attack, Why Can't FBI?" CNN, August 7, 2013.

228. Mark A. Thiessen, "Kidnapped Libyan Prime Minister Pays the Price for an Obama Leak," American Enterprise Institute, October 10, 2013.

229. Daniel Halper, "Hillary: We Must Empathize with America's Enemies," The Weekly Standard, December 4, 2014.

230. "Hillary Clinton Backer Jane Harman Questions Her Suggestion We 'Empathize' With Our 'Enemies,'" Washington Free Beacon, December 7, 2014.

231. Nick Milton, "What Is a Lesson Learned?" Knoco Stories, May 6, 2009.

232. Center for Army Lessons Learned.

233. Stephen M. Walt, "What Intervention in Libya Tells Us about the Neocon–Liberal Alliance," World News Daily, March 21, 2011.

234. "Libya's Cache of Toxic Arms All Destroyed," New York Times, February 2, 2014.

Index

Index